ENTREPRENEURSHIP IN INDIA'S SMALL-SCALE INDUSTRIES

ENTREPRENEURSHIP IN INDIA'S SMALL-SCALE INDUSTRIES
AN EXPLORATION OF SOCIAL CONTEXTS

Richard P. Taub and Doris L. Taub

R

The Riverdale Company
Riverdale, Maryland
1989

ISBN 0-913215-19-8

© Manohar Publications 1989
First Published 1989

Published in the United States of America
by The Riverdale Company, Publishers
Suite 102, 5506 Kenilworth Avenue,
Riverdale, Maryland 20737

by arrangement with Manohar Publications,
1 Ansari Road, Daryaganj, New Delhi - 110002,
Printed at P.L. Printers, C3/19 Rana Pratap Bagh,
Delhi - 110007, India

To two Neelas, Zach, and Chander

ACKNOWLEDGMENTS

We began the research for this book in 1971; after being interrupted by the war with Pakistan in December, 1971, we returned in the summer of 1972 to finish the first round of interviewing. In November and December 1975, we visited India once again to see how our respondents were doing in the face of worldwide recession and Mrs. Gandhi's proclamation of emergency rule five months earlier.

We were extremely fortunate in the help we received from our research assistants—in Tamilnadu, Mr. R.M.T. Sambandam and Ms. Neela Ramachandran; in Orissa, Dr. M.J. Iqbal, Mr. S.N. Patnaik, Mr. N. Venkat Swamy, and Mr. N. Pattabhi; and in Punjab, Mr. Ravi Sharma and Mr. Aswani Kumar Chopra. They performed with a high level of commitment and we profited enormously from their subtle and sensitive interpretations of life and culture.

In each state, too, we met people whose company informed our minds while enlivening our spirits: Messrs. S. Chockalingam, R. Radakrishnan, B. Venkatesan, and Ms. Shanta Bai in Tamilnadu; Messrs. N.R. Swamy, T.U. Vijayasekharan, N.M. Mahanty and S.C. Mahapatra in Orissa; Kartar and Kulwant Singh Birdi and Ranjit Singh Arora in Punjab. They nourished our spirits and—at least as important, as Indians understand so well—our bodies, and we are most grateful.

We were able as well to draw on the advice and counsel of some old friends: Messrs. J.P. Das, G.C. Somiah, Kartar Singh, T.N. Chaturvedi, J.B. Mathur, M. Narayanaswamy, B. Srinivasan, and K.S. Ramachandran, and we thank them for their willingness to chat through many cups of tea or coffee. In Chicago, our colleagues William Parish, Donald Levine, George Rosen, and Milton Singer stimulated and guided us.

Rick Bandstra and Harold McWilliams slogged with sensitivity, through countless hours of coding. Sara Lindholm and Bruce Stephenson provided skilled computer assistance. Ms. Lindholm also read the manuscript and commented on it critically. Kristen Day, Jackie Yu, Sophie Glazer, and Diane Durante all assisted with typing.

Funds for the research were given by the Fulbright Foundation, the American Institute of Indian Studies, and by the Committee on Southern Asian Studies and the Social Sciences Division of the University of Chicago. We are especially grateful to the University for its willingness to offer support in trying times.

Pradip Mehendiratta, Director of the Indian arm of the American Institute of Indian Studies, enabled us to complete our overfall 1975 program through his facilitation and support.

We must also thank our children, Neela and Zach, who suffered with grace the disruptions of travel when they might have preferred to be at home, and helped us to make many new friends.

Finally, we thank our more than two hundred respondents, many of whom are now our friends. They made our research a continuous adventure of discovery, and made it more pleasant and informative than was reasonable to expect.

R.P.T. and D.L.T.

Contents

CHAPTER ONE

INTRODUCTION

During the early 1970s, small-scale industry was the only Indian industrial sector in which substantial growth took place. Larger-scale industry grew at a rate scarcely above stagnation. Steel production never reached more than half of installed capacity. Agricultural output fell back from the early promise of the Green Revolution, rather more dependent on climatic conditions than its advocates had anticipated. Faced with stark shortages of materials and power, constrained by the elaborate sets of rules and restrictions that are part of India's conception of socialism, and frustrated by inadequate marketing facilities, small manufacturers nonetheless found niches for themselves in the interstices of a system geared to the workings of an almost inert government bureaucracy, large state-owned industries, and the giants of the private sector; and substantial numbers of them managed to thrive. Officials estimated the rate of small industry growth at about 10 per cent per annum. Growth continued at a rate only slightly diminished through the early 1980s. Although these figures are probably inflated—there are systematic reasons for overestimation of production that we will discuss later—there is little doubt that the growth of small-scale industries in India is a remarkable achievement.

Any social scientist interested in economic growth should be concerned about small industry in India for at least three reasons. First, small industries have played an important role in the development of the only highly industrialized non-Western country, Japan. The precise extent of their contribution is subject to debate, but, as in the Indian situation, a thriving small-scale sector grew in the interstices of Japan's well organized large industrial sector, both fueling it and supported by it, and provided a measure of vitality that at least two observers have considered crucial for Japan's economic growth (Okkawa and Rosovsky, 1973: 15; Hoselitz, 1968).

Second, the role of the entrepreneur in developing societies is a subject that is still being explored. Economic historians have painted entrepreneurs in heroic colors, in many instances giving them the principal credit for industrial growth in the West. Schumpeter defined as the function of entrepreneurship "to reform or revolutionize the pattern of production by exploiting an invention, or, more generally, an untried technological possibility for producing a new commodity or producing an old one in a new way, by opening up a new source of supply of material or a new outlet for products, by reorganizing an industry, and so on" (Schumpeter, 1942: 132). Arthur H. Cole, whose approach is closer to ours, included in his definition of entrepreneurs all those who "initiate, maintain, or aggrandize a profit oriented business unit for the production or distribution of economic goods and services" (Cole, 1959: 7). Cole also saw the entrepreneur as "the central figure in modern economic history, and, to [his] way of thinking, the central figure in economics" (Cole, 1965: 37). Many others (e.g. McClelland, 1966 and Hagan, 1971), too, have seen the growth of industrialization as a function of the quantity and quality of entrepreneurs available at a particular time. Increasing our understanding of entrepreneurs, therefore, is worthwhile for understanding the development process.

Further, the study of entrepreneurial activity in India may give special insights into the entrepreneurship question. A substantial body of literature argues that the effect of the Hindu religion on its practitioners is to make it difficult for them to become entrepreneurs (Kapp, 1963; Rose, 1970). This orientation gives us an opportunity, following Milton Singer (1973) and others, to explore how entrepreneurship is compatible with Hindu culture, and the sources of tension (if indeed there are any) arising from their alleged incompatibility. Doing so will help us understand better the nature of both entrepreneurship and Indian society.

Closely related to the question of entrepreneurship and industrialization is the question of modernization. The literature on modernization is rich and complex and, as with many rich and complex matters, confusion abounds. The theme that underlies the study of modernization is reflected in a famous colloquy between F. Scott Fitzgerald and Ernest Hemingway. "The rich are very different from you and me," began Fitzgerald. "Yes," Hemingway is supposed to have responded, "they have more money." The study of modernization has been the search for underlying qualitative differences between rich industrial nations (as distinct from those whose wealth comes from oil) and poor nonindustrial ones. The classic statement of the problem is Max Weber's: he asserts that "only in the West does science exist at a stage of development which we recognize as valid" (1958a: 13), and later, "the same is true of the most fateful force in our modern life, capitalism" (1958a: 17). He then goes on to ask "to what combination of circumstances the fact should be attributed that in Western civilization, and in Western civilization only, cultural phenomena have appeared which (as we like to think) lie in a line of development having universal significance and value" (1958a: 13).

Weber examined some of the major civilizations of the world looking for meaningful cultural differences. Social scientists after Weber—particularly in the post–World War II period—who observed differences in style between the inhabitants of the Western, industrialized countries and those in the nonindustrialized Third World, began to look systematically for those cultural differences that might be impediments to the development process. Almost all of the literature on modernization since then—with the significant exception of the literature attributing underdevelopment to exploitation of the Third World by Western imperialist countries—attempts to elaborate on those differences, emphasizing non-Western cultural styles themselves as hindrances to the development process. Among the differences between Western and non-Western styles to come under attack have been institutions such as family structure (families in nonindustrial countries include more generations and seem more dominated by authoritarian elders than those in the industrialized West [Goode, 1963]), value-patterned interactions (those in the nonindustrialized countries seem more particularistic, emphasizing ascription and functional diffuseness in their choice and quality of relationships [Parsons, 1961; Germani, 1968; and Levy, 1966]) and still others are social-psychological (people in the poorer countries supposedly lack empathy, flexibility, rational-manipulative orientations, and a desire to climb above their station [Lerner, 1964; Inkeles, 1966; and McClelland, 1966]). The word chauvinism has been debased by its persistent use as an epithet; yet, most of this literature is best characterized as chauvinistic. Running through it is an unselfconscious theme that highly values an idealized conception of Western behavior. In its more extreme form, the question this literature examines can be translated as "how can we get them to be more like us?"

Scholars espousing this "different is dysfunctional" view have seldom been able to specify precisely how their sociocultural variables relate causally to industrialization, and this is the crux of the problem. Implicitly, "modernization" is, in fact, the sociocultural correlate of industrialization. A "modern" society is one with a high gross national product, generated not through the sale of high priced natural resources (as in the oil producing states), but through the substantial increase in total resources that industrialization brings. This is so obviously true that even one of the most devoted followers of the "modernization equals changes in structure and values" school, Marion Levy, is forced to measure "modernization" by using indices that in fact measure industrialization: fossil fuel converted into energy, and effort multiplied by sophisticated tools. The question, then, is, are there social variables that are crucial for industrialization to occur? So far, the very question has been obscured, because those who see sociocultural variables as critical have not specified adequately how those variables relate causally to the process.

Functionalists have observed the closeness of fit between so-called modern cultural systems and industrialization (Goode, 1963; Levy, 1966). Others have seen cultural and social variables in a reciprocal relationship with industrialization: certain social and cultural variables encourage industrialization, which in turn encourages "modern" attitudes, structures, and behaviors, which then further encourage industrialization (Bendix, 1964 and, probably, Inkeles, 1974). Finally, some scholars have concluded that, to the extent that cultural and social-psychological modernization can be induced in individuals, economic development along the industrialization model is bound to take place (McClelland and Winter, 1968; Hagan, 1957).

The literature is confused, and often tries to avoid making this supposed relationship explicit. Scholars who work in these modes have difficulty distinguishing between micro- and macro-analysis—that is, moving from individual social-psychological levels to structural ones—and are unable to see the role that each level plays in the process. They also have difficulty distinguishing between deeply embedded, relatively unalterable cultural standards, internalized in individuals and reinforced by social structure, and those that can easily be changed—for example, by an increment in knowledge. Finally, even now—a time when cross-cultural sophistication has surely increased—these writers still have trouble distinguishing those aspects, if any, in the life of the modern industrial state that are essential to industrialization from those that are simply there, arising from the particular configuration of circumstances characteristic of the history of the West.

A less obvious problem with this literature (e.g. Inkeles) concerns the assumption that if one could identify a particular personality type that "fits" well with a "modern" set of social arrangements, the existence of that type in a society would necessarily conduce to the achievement of that set of arrangements where it had not existed previously. That is, if you reach a sufficient density of "modern men," they will help you to become modern. In other contexts, of course, we know that this model is inappropriate. A large body of well-documented data shows, for example, that builders of large industrial corporations in this country are not necessarily the best people to run them once they have become large. Innovators are often idiosyncratic and cantankerous; the very qualities that enable them to create new structures make them fit rather poorly in large ongoing organizations that need smoothly meshing parts.

Similarly, the persistent admiration in the literature for the nuclear family household type (Germani, Goode) seems inappropriate, given that many important Western industrializers were attached to complex extended families. We shall discuss this issue with respect to our Indian data in Chapter 10.

Similarly, taking a lead from Weber, others (e.g., Andreski, 1968) have emphasized the importance of asceticism and its beneficial effect on reinvestment. Weber even looked for ascetic business groups in India, and settled on the Jains as a potential functional equivalent of Calvinist Protestants. Yet again the concept of the "nouveaux riches" is precisely one of entrepreneurs who live lavishly as they build their wealth. Indeed, the opportunity to live lavishly is as important to them as the achievement of success itself, even though the price is to work heroic hours, pushing their employees as well; and for most, lavish living does not include the opportunity to relax.

Related to this set of issues, other pieces of baseline information need to be established. First, when one speaks of industrialization (or development, or modernization) in the Third World, one is not talking about initiating this process for the first time in the history of world experience. Even if it could be shown that a special personality and social configuration was important for the growth of industrialization in eighteenth century England, that is no reason to assume that the same forces are necessary for industrialization to occur in other countries in the twentieth century. In subsequent eras, the problem may simply become one of cultural diffusion: teaching people new techniques to organize capital, manufacture goods, and distribute them. That processes may differ at different historical periods has worked its way into the development literature. Gerschenkrohn, Bendix, and Moore, among others, have categorized developed nations on the basis of whether they came early or late to the process of development. Latecomers seem to be characterized by greater government participation in encouraging growth than early developers experienced. It may also be true, however, that different historical periods require different types of entrepreneurs.

We argue that in India, successful entrepreneurs defy identification with a particular set of sociocultural characteristics. Some live in extended families, some do not; some are ascetic, some are not; some hold to religious and social beliefs that would be called "modern" by the modernization theorists, and some hew much more closely to so-called traditional values and practices. The only generalization with which we feel comfortable is that the successful entrepreneurs segregate their beliefs about the nature of the world from their business practices, no matter what their ideology or rhetoric may be. In some cases, adherence to traditional social patterns facilitates achievement. Extended family households, for example, can provide both capital and a committed work force not available in the market at an affordable price. Devotion to religious practices gives one an appearance of trustworthiness that encourages others to do business with him. The refusal to limit the number of offspring ultimately provides a number of valued and trustworthy subordinates.

In other cases, entrepreneurs may jettison traditional forms, coming to look like the "modern men" of the modernization literature. Appearances, however, may be deceptive, since they may still hold to "traditional" beliefs in the spirit world, and doubt modern empirical science. These beliefs do not seem to impinge on their success. What does distinguish our successful industrialists from all the rest is their unswerving dedication to making money through business, combined with the application of all the rational principles at their command to that end.

What do we mean by "rational" in this context? First, we mean that our businessmen make those decisions they perceive as most likely to conduce to business success, given the options they believe are open to them. They do not, as some have argued, refuse to make an advantageous deal because the other party comes from the wrong caste or community. They may not organize their work or their activities according to Western principles of modern management, first, because they know their workers, the work setting, and what constitutes a reasonable demand on their workers given the setting; and second, because they may not be aware of all the options available to them. Many are not well educated; when confronted with a variety of options—particularly those considered the "latest" way to do something—they may not know how to make an optimal decision. This does not, however, mean that they are rigid, inflexible or unreceptive to change, as some of the literature (e.g., Inkeles) seems to suggest. To the contrary, successful entrepreneurs are quick to accept new alternatives when the connection between new methods and desired results is clear, and when the perceived potential cost of failing after trying new methods is moderate. Many entrepreneurs in India are in more economically precarious situations than are their American counterparts; this means that, being rational, they are less willing to take risks than they might be if they were more economically secure. A corollary of this is that small-scale industrialists get rapid feedback on the effects of their decisions and behaviors Nonrationalities find a more congenial home in large and complex organizations, because the effects of particular behaviors are more difficult to track, or to measure by their outcomes. In a large organization, outcomes are often far removed, both in people and in time, from the decisions and actions of initiators. For the official or manager of a large organization, small actions that please a superior may be more important to his career than outcomes far removed from decisions he makes. This is so true that much of both modern accounting theory and modern management theory involves pinning responsibility on managers for their role in producing distant final outcomes.

In a small organization, by contrast, feedback is often fast, and negative feedback may be immediately devastating. It took years for the Ford motor company to discover that making the Edsel was a bad decision, or for DuPont to make the same discovery about Corfam; and in neither case did a costly error seriously jeopardize the viability of the organization that made it. It takes only days, weeks, or months for a small industrialist to discover that there is no market for his product; or that the man he is dealing with is not reliable; or even that an older brother who, according to principles of family structure, ought to be the boss, is not good at making decisions.

We deliberately use American examples to make this point, because we do not want such difficulties in evaluating the consequences of organizational decisions written off as simply Indian problems.

It is true, of course, that the largest employer in India is the Indian government. Further, the government probably employs an unusually large number of individuals who would score high on a typical modernization scale. Yet, that organization is rife with the pathologies associated with large bureaucratic organizations (Taub, 1969), and more often allows areas of organizational nonrationality to exist, because the consequences are not immediately obvious.

One should add that small Indian companies, because they are not locked into large capital investments in outmoded equipment, and because they do not have large organizational structures filled with workers who have vested interests in continuing their behavior as before to protect themselves, are very much more flexible than larger ones. When feedback is negative, it is relatively easy for such an organization to turn around and do something else. At least one observer (Berna, 1960) has criticized small industrialists for changing their product lines frequently rather than developing them in depth. To make such a criticism is to fail to perceive the underlying similarity in technologies involved, which can be improved even while the manufacturer shifts products to those goods for which there is a market. The processes that go into making cycle cranks are the same as those required for making hand tools; a company that can move easily from one to another as demand shifts is actually in a very strong position. The small industrialist hence has more opportunities to make rational decisions in his business behavior than does either a large manufacturer or a government official.

That this is so may not always be apparent to the foreign observer, because the rhetoric many Indian businessmen use to explain their behavior suggests otherwise. Asked why he chose a particular occupation, a respondent may say that it is his traditional one; or that it is hereditary in his family. He may mean simply that his father did it before him—and not necessarily very much before him, as with a manufacturer of camphor tablets, whose "traditional" occupation began when his father took it up twelve years ago. Contrary to what people may say, the range of occupational choices open is large; individuals who appear to be tradition-bound usually are nothing of the kind.

What we have suggested so far is that the often ignored core problem of modernization is in fact the process of industrialization; it may, therefore, be inappropriate to look for a "modern" value complex in individuals to determine who the modernizers are and what the potential for subsequent development is, and that the production of more modern men is also not an especially desirable means to encourage the process. For if one looks at the industrializers themselves, one discovers that the "modern" value complex is largely irrelevant to understanding the quality of their performance. This, however, is only half the problem. We still must find the links between the phenomenon of individual entrepreneurial success and societal economic growth. It may well be true that the presence of many successful small entrepreneurs does not necessarily translate into national growth. Just as it may be possible to have economic growth without any entrepreneurs in the formal sense at all, as the Soviet Union and the Republic of China have demonstrated, it may also be true that one could have many entrepreneurs but little economic growth because something in their environment blunts their efforts.

In other settings, the environment may be able to multiply entrepreneurial efforts, as has happened in twentieth century Japan. If we can begin to look at the problem, we can start to construct links between micro- and macro-structures, an effort usually absent in the literature on development; scholars concentrate on one or the other. Environment can enter into the process in different ways. One reason France lagged behind England in early industrial growth was that it encouraged the manufacture of luxury goods rather than mass-market goods, consequently limiting the speed and volume of growth in production.

Widespread hostility toward the process of earning money through business may have negative consequences. Where attitudes toward doing business are strongly negative, young men may not aspire to achievement through that route; fathers may earn wealth in industry so they can retire to agricultural lands, and discourage their offspring from following in their footsteps.

Hostility towards business may be translated into state policy. Confiscatory taxation, elaborate and time-consuming controls, and the discouragement of credit can all set limits on an entrepreneur's potential achievement.

This list is not meant to be exhaustive, but only to suggest possibilities. The point is that one way to move from micro- to macro-structures may be through considering the environments in which entrepreneurs must function.

Toward that end, we wish to take initial steps in understanding the environments in which small industries in India operate. One major concern here is the exploration and evaluation of the Government of India program explicitly aimed at producing the growth of small-scale industries. This program provides inducements—cheap credit, low rent facilities, and subsidized raw materials; facilitators—technical expertise and advice; and "positive thinking" through exhortation. We shall look at the program in a variety of settings to understand better the impact of other environmental aspects as well.

In so doing we explicitly alter our orienting framework from a concern with the nature of entrepreneurship to problems related to the difficulties of organizing planned social change.

Governments, government agencies, and other corporate groups frequently seek to induce their members to change their behavior in some important way, often to help solve problems pertinent to economic growth. Yet these efforts—motivating farmers to use improved seeds, poor people to have fewer children, young people to stay in school longer, workers to rationalize their systems of work, employees to be nice to clients or otherwise to alter their accustomed habits of work, doctors to establish practices outside of cities, and developers to build urban housing for poor people—are all enterprises that have turned out to be surprisingly difficult to accomplish.

The literature about such attempts around the world is replete with reports of failure. In this regard, the Indian case is particularly interesting, for in some states, small industries are growing rapidly—as we have noted already, the small-scale sector is a growing one in India—and in others, it is not growing at all. This provides an opportunity to weigh the impact of the program as compared to other environmental forces. Toward that end, let us turn to the Government of India's Small Industries Development Program. We will then look at the industries themselves in three Indian states: Punjab, where small-scale industrial growth has been dramatic; Tamilnadu, where such growth has been steady but unspectacular; and Orissa, where there has been no growth to speak of.

Having reviewed the small industries program in India, we will then look at small-scale industrial activities in each state, compare them, and then consider the entrepreneurs against the background of modernization theory. We then analyze the impact of the small industries program on these individuals, and how different types of entrepreneurs use it in each state. Finally, we try to show how characteristics of entrepreneurs connect to characteristics of the society in which they find themselves, and we try to predict on that basis how individual entrepreneurs will intersect with societal activity as a whole in the near future.

CHAPTER TWO

THE SMALL-SCALE INDUSTRIES PROGRAM: HISTORY AND GOALS

What is a Small-Scale Industry?

A small-scale industry in India is not merely what one might intuitively think it to be. It is, in addition, an entity officially if ambiguously defined by the Government of India as an industrial unit having a specified ceiling on investment in machinery and materials. At the time of our study, that ceiling was Rs. 750,000 (GOI, DCSSI, n.d.a.: 56). By 1980, that figure had been increased in response to inflation to Rs. 2 million (Vepa, 1983). Ancillary industries—those that manufacture parts principally for one larger industry under a long-term contract—could in the 1970s have an investment up to Rs. 1 million (GOI, DCSSI, n.d.a.: 54–55), a figure that by 1980 had been raised to Rs. 2.5 million. Since investment in land, factory buildings (or sheds, as they are called in India), and warehouse facilities (godowns) are excluded from this calculation, enterprises that are officially classed as small scale can clearly be very large indeed.

At the other end of the scale, no minimum investment is necessary before a producing unit qualifies as a small-scale industry. This omission has two consequences: first, obviously, the range in size and complexity of small-scale units is enormous; and second, it is often difficult—for official as well as scholarly purposes—to distinguish adequately among "small-scale" industries, "cottage" or "village" industries, and "handicrafts." While government officials have some notion about what constitutes a "real" small-scale industry and what falls into the other two categories (see, e.g., Alexander, n.d.: 38), the guidelines are neither clearly formulated nor consistently applied. Hence, for example, people who carve utilitarian and decorative objects from animal horn, those who make pots out of bell metal, and others whom we shall call traditional craftsmen are included in some states as small-scale industrialists, whereas handloom weavers are not. Indeed, the notion of *producing* something is not integral to the concept of small-scale industry. Most government officials to whom we spoke agreed that in principle one ought to consider only manufacturers as industries (the exception here was the Director of Industries for Orissa, who included those producing either goods or services). When a service enterprise uses machinery, and particularly if the machinery is electrically powered, then that enterprise too may be considered a small-scale "industry." In consequence, those using lathes to make repairs, electrical repair shops, dry cleaning establishments, and job printers were all included as small-scale industries in the official rosters of one or more of the states we studied.

Because of our interest in the relationship between government small industries programs and the condition of the industries themselves, we decided to use the government definition of what constitutes a small-scale industry rather than formulate a more rigorous definition of our own, or one that conformed more closely to our sense of what one *ought* to mean when referring to a small industry.

Even given the considerations we have just discussed, it is difficult for a Western reader, raised on stories of Henry Ford and images of assembly lines, and taught, because of our own economic realities, that production costs are lowered through the substitution of mechanical for human labor, to flesh out the official definition and visualize in his mind's eye the organization and operation of small-scale (and, indeed, many larger-scale) industries in India. Let us try to put some meat on the official bones.

At one end of the spectrum is the technologically rudimentary industry, in which sheet metal workers count heavily. A typical sheet metal worker, listed officially as a manufacturer of trunks (used in India in place of bureaus for the storage of clothes) or buckets or drums or steel furniture for offices and hospitals, works in an earthen-floored shed made of sticks and mud or corrugated metal, perhaps four feet square. His raw materials are sheets of metal—often, used oil drums—and his tools a hammer. He manufactures his product by hammering and bending the metal until he has fashioned, by hand, the desired item.

At the other extreme are industries producing technologically sophisticated products in spacious, well lighted sheds made of cement blocks or poured concrete on the industrial estates and in newly developed industrial areas. Among the items manufactured in such locations are ball bearings, electronic counting and sorting equipment, fine tolerance plastic parts for automobiles, and 70-millimeter projection equipment for the elegant movie houses of New Delhi, Bombay, and other cities. Even here, however, there are no assembly lines, and little machinery in relation to the number of workers. We did not, however, see the throngs of idle workers standing around aimlessly that some other scholars have observed (Myers, 1958; Rice, 1958). Our impression is that some of the larger industries in India keep extra labor on hand much as large American industries stockpile spare parts for their machines; but in our own sample, we were struck by the purposiveness of most workers' behavior.

Each mechanical process alters the material only a little. A worker puts a steel bar through a machine that trims its edges to make it hexagonal. Another worker cuts a small piece from the bar and passes it to a third, who drills a hole through it. A fourth worker threads the piece. The result is a nut. Few factories have dies that produce identical parts without human intervention; machine-made parts have rough edges that require finishing. Although this changed somewhat during the years of our study, owners might employ ten workers using hand files to finish parts rather than do the work mechanically. Lathes and grinders often do not have jigs that preset them to desired tolerances automatically. Consequently, most manufacturing jobs require some measure of worker skill and judgment, because few of the processes are completely routinized. There are exceptions, of course: a machine that stamps bicycle fenders requires a worker only to feed in flat strips of metal, and power looms (those horrors of nineteenth-century England) require frequent tending but little judgment—a single worker can look after three or four of them.

In general, however, not only must workers interpose themselves in the manufacturing process, but—within limits set by the needs of other workers for the item that will be passed on, and the constraints set by bosses and supervisors who want to keep output up—they control the pace of their own work. Even sophisticated machines do not usually run automatically, but must first be set up by the worker, and then activated by him when all is ready. Hence the work flow is slower and less smooth than in a typical American factory (and the workers less like automatons), the more so because adjacent stages in the manufacturing process often are not physically adjacent in the shed; other considerations, such as the shape of the building, the location of electrical connections, and the position of a drive belt or pulley may determine where different operations will be carried out.

Between the extremes of precision products manufactured in the modern sheds on the industrial estate and the rudimentary consumer goods produced in tiny shacks on back alleys lies an enormous range of commodities fabricated in many types of workplace. Among them are textile products made on power looms and knitting machines set up in the manufacturer's livingroom; traditional cigarettes produced by subcontracted laborers in their villages; small boats fabricated in a large yard on the water's edge; a tobacco-flavored toothpaste mixed and canned in the compound (courtyard) of an elegant house situated on an acre of property (over which the ingredients are spread out to dry); sewing machines assembled in a succession of factory rooms located alongside an open drain; plastic parts injection-molded on six machines housed in a tiny corrugated shed on a corner of another spacious compound; hydraulic presses made in a large modern factory from freshly imported machine tools that stand in rows, purring quietly, tended by at least two full-time workers whose sole responsibility is to oil them and polish their chrome; and so on.

Underlying this great diversity, however, is a common thread of basic manufacturing processes—stamping, machining, casting, mixing, weaving. These producers' expertise lies in their mastery of these skills, rather than in their knowledge of or commitment to the particular product they may be manufacturing at a given time. A number of our respondents have changed their product several times, a phenomenon that some observers (e.g., Berna, 1960) have incorrectly identified as nonrational behavior. Quite the contrary, skill in a particular type of manufacturing process gives the producer the flexibility to respond to the exigencies of changing conditions of raw materials supply and markets that no small Indian manufacturer can afford to ignore if he hopes to remain in business for long.

The extent of profitability of the industries is nearly as variable as the range of their products. An earlier study of small-scale industries (McCrory, 1956) equated "small-scale" and "marginal," and in fact most of the firms reported on in that study did fail. Our sample, by contrast, ranged from industries that had already failed by the

time of interview to those that were highly profitable, with the
majority providing at least what the owner defined as "a good
income"; that is, more than he could earn working for someone
else.

Interpreting Available Statistics

It is easy enough on the scene to learn a lot about individual
small-scale industries. Acquiring information about them in the
aggregate, however, is another matter altogether. Statistics about
small-scale industries are scarce, and those that are available are
unreliable. Government definitions of what constitutes a small-
scale industry have changed from time to time, but more important, the small size of many enterprises, the large number of them,
and their geographical dispersion have made it very difficult to
track them down. Registration of small-scale units is required, but
"on a voluntary basis" (GOI, DCSSI, n.d.a: 206), which means in
practice that those firms that want something from the government,
as well as those that have inadvertently come to the government's
attention (perhaps by applying for indemnification after communal riots, or by being located next to another industry visited by a
government officer), register, and the remainder do not.

Optimistic government officials, especially central government
officials who are far removed from the field, like to assume that
"almost all the small-scale units get themselves registered with the
State Directorates of Industries . . ." (GOI, DCSSI, n.d.a.: 205), but on-
the-ground observation suggests that many units—especially the
smaller ones whose requirements are few, or more importantly,
who feel that they do not know how to deal with the government
and therefore will never be able to get what is due them—do not,
bother to register. Conservative government officials have estimated the number of unregistered units at about 250,000 (e.g.,
Nanjappa, n.d.: iii), but gave no clue about how they arrived at that
figure. Only a complete census of small-scale industries would
yield a reliable index of the number of unregistered units, but the
costs of such a census are too great for most state budgetmakers to
contemplate.

Many small-scale industrialists consciously avoid registering
until they cannot get along without some good or service that only
the government can provide. They are in general suspicious of the
government and do not want officials "meddling" or telling them
what to do. In addition, almost everyone is breaking at least one

law: underreporting income to the tax authorities, trading in the black market, employing more workers than he reports, or using younger workers than is legally permitted. Consequently, few people welcome the entrance of the government into their lives. Some of these strategies are necessary for industries to function at all; but their effect on the collection of even the most basic statistics about small-scale industries—how many there are, what their output and profits are, how many people they employ, their capital investment—is disastrous. It is simply impossible at present to make any reliable estimate on most of these dimensions (cf. Ahmed, n.d.: 5).

Even seemingly bedrock figures rest on shifting sands. The most often quoted statistic about small-scale industries is that in 1969, 178,000 units were registered with the government (GOI, DCSSI, n.d.b: 721). Since that figure is simply a total of registrations in each state, one might think it reliable. But what goes into that compilation of registrations? States lagging behind in industrial development register almost any enterprise that produces something or uses a motor, and some enterprises that do neither. Thus, the Orissa *Directory of Industries* (Government of Orissa, 1967) included people who make clothing by hand and people who make stamp blocks by hand. A man who repaired harmoniums (a musical instrument in the accordion family) was listed in the Orissa *Directory* not once but three times. Further, many of these units were "registered" without the knowledge of the owners.

Cooperative societies and workshops run by the state were included in the listings of registered small-scale industries in all the state directories we examined. So were fraudulent industries—established to be eligible for low price raw materials allocations that they could sell at the much higher market rate—which have never produced anything at all. So were defunct industries, since the government was much more efficient at adding the names of new industries to its rolls than in removing out-of-business ones.

Finally, an indeterminate number of enterprises was included that formally met all the criteria for a small-scale industry but did not fit the larger conception of small-scale units as independent entrepreneurship in action. These were the industries established by larger-scale manufacturers as, in effect, wholly-owned subsidiaries of the larger concern. Manufacturers set these units up because they could then take advantage of some of the benefits available to small-scale units, such as more liberal labor laws and tax advantages. They did not, however, represent a new or additional contribution to the industrial economy, and in that sense their inclusion in statistics on small-scale sector growth, in numbers, output, or whatever, is misleading.

Further complicating the statistical question is the method used by the government to report data. Figures for small-scale industries were often, though not always, aggregated with those for other types of units, leading to reporting in categories such as "Small-Scale and Village Industries." The handicrafts industries included as "Village Industries" are separate from the small-scale industries in principle, policy, and practice. They are administered separately from the small-scale industries, are not beneficiaries of the small-scale industries program, and hence should be excluded from our consideration. They are not, however, separate in much of the government's statistical reporting. Since there was no way to estimate from such figures the component contributed by the small-scale sector alone, aggregate statistics of this type were useless for our purposes.

Given these limitations, one does not quite know what to make of official figures. Total output for the small-scale sector in 1970 has been reported as Rs. 36.7 billion based on a capital investment of Rs. 23.28 billion (Vepa, 1971: 25), but both true output and true capital investment were almost certainly higher because of under-enumeration by the government and underreporting by producers. By 1981, that figure had reportedly risen to Rs. 280.8 billion (Vepa, 1983: 2). The reported small-scale output is estimated to constitute a little over a third of India's total industrial output (Nanjappa, n.d.: iii), and the small-scale output sector is said variously to employ 40 per cent (Vepa, 1971: 25) or 50 per cent (Nanjappa, n.d.: iii) of the workers in the Indian industrial labor force. Whatever be the shortcomings of these estimates, they are a guide to the orders of magnitude involved; but one should remember that offical statistics reported as precise numbers should be taken as a rough approximation to reality at best.

History of the Small-Scale Industries Program

The development of the small-scale industrial sector has been a stated national goal since Independence. The Industrial Policy Resolution of 1948 outlined the role that the small-scale sector might play in contributing to the national output, providing employment, and developing backward areas, and enunciated a policy of encouragement to small industry through government provision of raw materials (including power), technical advice, marketing assistance, and protection from "intensive competition" from large-scale industry (GOI, 1948: 3295-96, 3392-93). The scant funds allocated to small industry in the First Five-Year Plan, however—Rs. 50 million of a total plan allocation of Rs. 42 billion (Vepa, 1971: 16)—demonstrated that the real emphasis in early post-Independence India was to be on heavy industry and agriculture, with small industry taking a distinctly backseat role. Consonant with the lack of funding provided, few steps were taken during the first plan period to implement any of the policies toward small industry that had been formulated in 1948.

In late 1953, the Ford Foundation sponsored an international study group field inspection and assessment of the condition of small-scale industries in India. The study group observed that "the rate of development of small industries is. . . slow. . . . Many small industries are now facing a crisis, deteriorating in ouput and employment. . . . (Ford Foundation, 1955: 1). The study team recommended creating a specialized small-scale sector in industry and multipurpose institutes to serve it; establishing agencies to provide the small producer, expeditiously and with minimal red tape, with both credit and working capital; promoting trade associations and industrial cooperatives; and offering government assistance in marketing (Ford Foundation, 1955).

The Ford Foundation report served as a rallying point for officials in the Government of India who had been urging implementation of the policy propounded in 1948, and the program was set in motion. Allocations for small-scale industry proposed for the Second Five-Year Plan 1956-61) jumped from the earlier Rs. 50 million, which had constituted about one-eighth of one per cent of the first plan budget, to Rs. 610 million of a total Rs. 60 billion, or slightly over one per cent of the entire budget for the Second Plan (Vepa, 1971: 17-18). A central government Small-Scale Industries Board was established in 1954 as a top-level advisory body making recommendations directly to the Ministry of Industrial Development and Company Affairs, and with responsibility for overall planning, coordination, and development of small-scale industries and the programs aimed at them (GOI, DCSSI, n.d.a: 28-29, 61). The founding of these agencies marked the formal commencement of the Small-Scale Industries Program, and the initiation of the policy distinction between "small-scale" industries and "cottage" or "village" industries and handicrafts.

Soon thereafter, the Government of India adopted the Industrial

Policy Resolution of 1956 (GOI, Planning Commission, 1956: 433–39), which enunciated a policy of increased emphasis on development of the small-scale sector. The expanded policy of support—now backed by funding to insure its implementation—included concessional levels of taxation for and direct subsidies to small enterprises, and restrictions on the volume of production to be permitted to competitive large-scale units (GOI, Planning Commission, 1956: 437).

By 1964, when the international study team returned, they found an enormously expanded government presence in the small-scale sector. Numerous agencies, under both central government and state aegis, having diverse facilitating functions at every level of small industrial organization and management, had been established. In response, the study team focused in its second report on problems in the administration of the program as it had come to be, rather than on recommendations for still newer institutional arrangements. While observing that "the prospects for modern small factories . . . are bright" (Ford Foundation, 1964: 1), the team singled out problems of raw materials acquisition as a major obstacle to their continued development. Small industries, they said,

> are presently seriously handicapped in comparison with larger units by an inequitable allocation system for scarce raw materials and imported components. . . . Due to the segmented government allocation system, allocations to small units are generally lower, in relation to total capacity, than allocations to larger firms producing the same products. . . ; divisions of allocations among the States is not in any sense based on scientific judgements related to development goals; and. . . allocations to individual firms by State directors of industries (based on assessed capacities for some prior year. . . with little regard to present capacity or importance of product to the national economy) are not based on any uniformly-applied logical system.
>
> As a consequence, small units have to buy a larger share of their requirements at higher prices on the black market than do large units, and are therefore at a competitive disadvantage. Also, despatches to small firms are more uncertain and erratic and less related to needs than those of their large-scale competitors. . . (Ford Foundation, 1964: 2).

We have quoted this appraisal at length because the problems pointed to in 1964 had become even more acute by 1971. Ironically, shortages of raw materials became more severe in part precisely because of the increasing vigor of the small-scale sector. This situation began to change in 1975 when the government invoked emergency powers to root out "black money" and reduce labor "indiscipline." The results were, on the one hand, recession in the small-scale sector (which had been heavily dependent on the availability of black money) and a concurrent increase in output of steel mills (which had been strike-prone), leading to a new congruence between demand for materials and available supply.

The second theme recurring throughout the report is that of the need for greater focus and concentration of resources on selected aspects of the program. The team urged the government to conserve foreign exchange while increasing production by importing raw materials, to be fabricated with existing equipment, rather than importing new equipment (Ford Foundation, 1964: 2-3). The report further emphasized the need to use program resources to provide high quality technical assistance to existing units, rather than trying simply to increase the number of units (particularly since adequate technical assistance could not be provided to more units) (1964: 3). Finally, the team recommended concentrating support on those industrialists and locations that demonstrated the greatest probability of contributing to national economic development, rather than dispersing efforts and resources equally among those who could and those who could not use them productively. Many of these recommendations were equally applicable at the time of our research. They had not been implemented because the government had been unable to decide among conflicting goals for small-scale industry.

Since 1964, the Small-Scale Industries Program has continued to receive government attention, and institutions and facilities devoted to serving the small-scale sector have grown accordingly. The Third Five-Year Plan (1961-66) allocation to the program was Rs. 1.14 billion of an overall plan expenditure of Rs. 105 billion (Vepa, 1971: 19), again about one per cent of the total. This plan was the first to reserve specified articles—all of them plastic or polyester—for production exclusively by the small-scale sector, a program that has continued to expand. The Fourth Five-Year Plan, which was to have covered 1969 through 1974, collapsed and was replaced with a series of Annual Plans. The plan for 1970-71 again called for an expenditure of about one per cent (more than Rs. 203 million of a total Rs. 28.2 billion) (GOI Planning Commission, 1971: 7, 122) on small-scale industries.

Goals

What does the Government of India hope to accomplish through the development of small-scale industries? The Industrial Policy Resolution of 1948, which was the first statement of goals the government hoped to achieve through small-industrial growth, set the tone for future policy. It saw in small industries a means for better using local resources and for achieving local self-sufficiency in essential consumer goods (the idea of the virtue of village and hand industry is one of the several Gandhian themes that run through the policy rationale); a means for alleviating unemployment, and in particular for rehabilitating refugees from the areas that became Pakistan after Partition; a provider of opportunity for individual, village, and cooperative enterprise; a means to increase production in the face of limitations on the availability of capital goods for large-scale industry; and, an opportunity to attend to the economic and social needs of the common man in the village (GOI, 1948: 3295–96, 3392–93).

The aims of increasing employment and developing the national economy were reiterated in the Industrial Policy Resolution of 1956, and some new goals for the program were added. The growth of small-scale industries, it was expected, would ensure a more equitable distribution of national income; provide balanced industrial development among all regions of the country (without which a general increase in the standard of living for all citizens was thought to be impossible); facilitate an effective mobilization of resources, both of capital and of entrepreneurial and managerial skill, that might otherwise remain unused; and mitigate problems of "unplanned urbanisation" by establishing "small centres of industrial production all over the country" (GOI, 1956: 436–37), this last another legacy of Gandhi, who had written with abhorrence of the evils of urban life. All of these goals, policymakers supposed, would be accomplished with minimal expenditure— small-scale industry is imagined to be "labour-intensive and capital-saving" (Ahmed, n.d.: 3)—for maximum return.

These themes have been sounded again and again by high-level government officials. A.K. Roy, then Joint Secretary in the Ministry of Industrial Development and Company Affairs, wrote in 1968 that

> small-scale industries are being developed in India. . . since they
> fulfill two important objectives of economic development.
> Firstly, they facilitate the decentralisation of economic power by

encouraging prospective entrepreneurs from middle levels of society to take up industrial ventures and also help in the dispersal of industries over the entire geographic area of the country. Secondly, they facilitate the transformation of traditional technology characterised by low skill, low productivity and low wages into modern technology characterised by improved skill, high productivity and rising wages (n.d.: 28).

Or consider this extract from a paper written by R. Venkataraman, a Member of the Planning Commission:

> [C]onsumer demand . . . was planned to be met substantially by development of small industries, which, on the one hand, do not make heavy demand on scarce capital resources, and, on the other hand, provide increasing employment opportunities.
>
> In a country like India with vast distances and a large potential market, there are other important reasons also which weigh in favour of development of small industries as well as decentralisation and dispersal of industries. Development of small industries facilitates effective mobilisation of resources of capital and skill particularly in the countryside, which might otherwise remain unutilised. These industries also offer a method of promotion of new entrepreneurs and of ensuring a more equitable distribution of the national income (n.d.: 3).

These statements represent a confusion of desired goals with concrete accomplishments. No systematic data have been marshaled to date to show that the development of small industry in India has led to decentralization of economic power or a more equitable distribution of income, encouraged prospective entrepreneurs, helped in the dispersal and decentralization of industry, or mobilized rural resources of capital and skill. Our own data suggest that some of these goals are being accomplished, but often at the expense of others.

Clearly, the official view of the development of the small-scale sector has from the beginning been that it will provide a cheap solution to many of the country's most vexing problems. And there lies the rub. Broadly, the program since its inception has had both economic and social goals. Although official statements have attempted to reconcile them, the two are often incompatible. To the extent that the government has been unable to determine its priorities, achieving either has been hindered.

Let us consider two examples. The development of industrial

estates—planned industrial areas that include factory sheds and electrical and water supplies—was one of the first parts of the Small-Scale Industries Program to be implemented, and, as Vepa observes, "the Industrial Estates were successful initially so that the programme expanded rapidly and, perhaps, almost indiscriminately" (1971: 18). By the end of 1967, 486 industrial estates had been approved, but of these only 231 were completed and in use. An additional 105 estates had been completed but were not functioning and the remainder were still under construction (Roy, n.d.: 30–31). By 1969, these proportions remained unchanged. Another 25 estates had been completed, for a total of 361, and the number of non functioning estates had grown to 113 (Srinivasan, 1970: 29). Some of the estates lacked water or electricity or both; construction on others was stalled; and in others that had been completed, not a single building was being used.

We believe there was nothing "indiscriminate," in a policy sense, about the growth of industrial estates. Official policy assumed, almost ideologically, that wherever such resources were offered, social benefits would result. Political reality created pressure to assure the widest provision of such boons ("If they get one, we want one"), even where there was no user demand. Officials charged with implementation wanted to leave their mark in office. All these combined to make the outcome overdetermined. We saw the process in action in Orissa in 1971. The state Director of Industries talked to us enthusiastically about his aspiration to provide an industrial estate for every district in Orissa. Yet just a few miles from his office, the Cuttack district industrial estate—located in Orissa's most populous and industrialized district—was only half filled. There is no question that extensive public resources that could have been put to good use in any of a number of other ways have gone to construct facilities that might decay before sufficient demand arose (or was stimulated) to take advantage of them.

The second example concerns who gets help from the government through the Small-Scale Industries Program. A major thrust of all the policy statements has been that the small man must be mobilized, his managerial skills and his capital unleashed, and his contribution to industrial development secured, for both his own good and that of the nation. Yet our observation is that the unlettered, impecunious industrialist at whom so many efforts are in principle aimed is precisely the one who cannot get past the gatekeeper in the offices of government officials ostensibly there to help him. In practice, officials are much more sympathetic to the educated, technically trained, middle-class industrialists who, not coincidentally, are more like themselves. After all the rhetoric about providing a solution to rural unemployment, the bulk of the resources goes to the urbanized middle and upper-middle class. While our view is that helping the prosperous entrepreneur probably will have more long-term payoff for the economy of India—and consequently, for all the people—than does helping the "common man," this bias, reflected in official action, certainly is counter to the expressed aims of mobilizing rural resources of skill and capital and recruiting new entrepreneurs.

The Ford Foundation team, as long ago as 1964, had no such ambivalence about the role that the small-scale sector in India ought to play. They saw small industry as an integral part of India's program for economic development. If social gains could be derived, well and good; but they saw no issue about the need to subordinate short-range social benefits to long-range industrial development:

> In combination with other factors, industrial estates can be helpful in stimulating industrial growth where adequate space and facilities are not otherwise available at reasonable cost. However, India's experience has abundantly proved that estates alone cannot overcome locational disadvantages. The experience should be taken into account when locating new estates. On this basis, it is recommended that all further proposals for industrial estates or workshops to be financed by public funds should be reviewed for economic viability by the CSIO (Central Small Industries Organisation) before plans are approved (1964: 10).

And further:

> Industrial dispersal programs are desirable from many points of view, and India's planners are quite correct in adopting them in principle. However, small industry promotion should not be regarded as the sole or even the major means of achieving the desired spread of industry. . . . Artificial measures to encourage the growth of industrial units . . . at uneconomic locations can only put additional strain on national financial, transport, educational, and other resources without commensurate benefit. Any immediate social or political advantages that may accrue from dispersal decisions made for reasons that ignore economic fac-

tors are likely to be offset many-fold, even in the communities initially benefited. We therefore urge careful economic analysis before making location decisions in order that the total national costs may be correctly evaluated in relation to the benefits received and to the effect on accelerated national development. It is particularly evident that a policy of trying to implant large amounts of industry in the most backward areas or directly in villages is doomed to failure and cannot be justified economically. Instead, secondary areas and centres should be selected that have inherent locational advantages to become potential growth points for industry . . . (1964: 12–13).

On the subject of who should be helped by the Small-Scale Industries Program, the study team had these comments:

An attempt has been made to provide too many services, in too many locations, for the available resources of trained men and equipment. There should be greater concentration of activity in major locations, and for those industries where the maximum contribution can be made to national growth objectives.

Priority should therefore be given to helping, in depth, those industrialists who have the inherent capability for progressive growth in industries that are most important to the economic development of the country (1964: 6).

Despite these criticisms, the Government of India—caught between conflicting policy goals and political pressure—has so far been unable to steer a straight course toward the achievement of either set of goals.

The Small-Scale Industries Program

The Small-Scale Industries Programme adopted by us is acknowledged as one of the most comprehensive of its type. The small industrialist is assured of assistance at all stages— from decision to set up an industrial unit to the marketing of the finished products—and of all types—financial, technical, managerial, and marketing (Nanjappa, n.d.: iv).

So wrote K.L. Nanjappa, then Development Commissioner Small-Scale Industries, in his introduction to a volume prepared by the Government of India celebrating its achievements in the small industry realm. It is the kind of statement that high officials—far removed from the exigencies of implementing programs—are fond of making; and indeed, at the policy level, the Small-Scale Industries Program is, as government programs anywhere go, exceptionally well designed. Let us follow a hypothetical entrepreneur in 1975 through an ideal-typical path from selection of industry to marketing of product, to see what, in principle, the program provides.

From the viewpoint of a prospective industrialist, the program reached out to him even before he decided to set up. The government sponsored small industries fairs and exhibitions, complete with rides, sideshows, music, and other amusements to complement the display of products made by small industry in each of the states. Between fairs, the state Departments of Industries advertised in newspapers and on the radio, emphasizing the opportunity that owning an industry presented for earning great sums, and describing the services available for small industrialists.

Once a prospective entrepreneur had decided that setting up an industry seemed a good idea, the government was prepared to assist him all the way. The state Small Industries Service Institute was in principle ready with advice on the prospects for various industries, data on marketing potential, and suggestions for how to choose a site, and had handbooks—over one thousand of them—giving the details for setting up particular industries (Nanjappa, n.d.: v). Handbook titles included: "Panel Pins and Wire Nails," "Cast-Iron Metric Weights," "Hand-Molded Fire Bricks and Special Refractory Shapes," "Shuttlecocks," "Braided Cords and Tapes with Elastic Threads," "Type-Foundry," "Artificial Teeth from Methyl Methacrylate," "Crushed Bones for Export," "Cutlery Items," "Black Tapes for Electrical Wiring," "Fireworks Factory," "Optical Equipment," "Poultry Appliances," "Magnasite Nozzles," "Card Board Slates," "Crank Shaft Forgings," "Gang Operated Air Brake Switch," and "Gland Packing for Locomotive Piston Rods." Also available were general "how-to-do-it" booklets, such as "Right Leather for Right Jobs," "Applications of Jigs and Fixtures," and "Blue-Black Writing Ink—Its Manufacture Troubles and Remedies." An entrepreneur might give special consideration to manufacturing one of the "Items Reserved Exclusively for Production in the Small-Scale Sector" by the government (GOI, DCSSI, n.d.b: 621). In 1975, there were 75 such items; by 1980, this figure had risen to 500.

Having selected his industry, the entrepreneur could choose his site. If he lived near an industrial estate, he might consider renting a shed there. Sheds in the industrial estates were built for short-term rental and eventual sale at concessional prices to their renters, although state governments became reluctant to part with the sheds, even where—as in Madras city—tenants pressured the government to do so.

The entrepreneur's next problem was likely to be financing for the purchase of raw materials and equipment. Depending on the size of the loan he needed, the entrepreneur could go to his District Industries Officer, state Financial Corporation, his state Small Industries Corporation, the state Industrial Development Corporation, or to a bank. The banking system was not formally incorporated into the Small-Scale Industries Program because until 1969 most banks in India were not government owned. One impetus to nationalization of the banks, in fact, was to free more capital for loans to small industry. Following nationalization, lending policies toward small producers were liberalized somewhat, but the banks—partly because it costs as much to process a small loan as a large one, and partly because of the greater risks involved in lending to small entrepreneurs—preferred to give funds earmarked for small industry loans to industrialists at the upper end of the small scale. To counter the "high risk" argument, the National Small Industries Corporation had begun guaranteeing bank loans to small industrialists (Roy, n.d.: 33).

If an industrialist did not have the necessary security to take a large loan, he could buy machinery through the hire-purchase (installment buying) program offered by the National Small Industries Corporation (NSIC) or, in some states (e.g., Haryana), through the state's Small Industry Corporation. For earnest money of 20 per cent of the machine's purchase price, the NSIC would order the machine and pay for it. The industrialist had to repay the price of the machine over 7 years at a concessional interest rate.

If the entrepreneur's chosen industry required raw materials in scarce supply (and almost all were: among the items on the government's list of controlled materials in 1971 were iron and steel, non-ferrous metals, chemicals including those for foodstuffs, plastics, optical glass, and wool; at other times, the list has included rubber, cement, sugar, and foodgrains), he might have wanted to apply to the government for an allocation of raw materials at controlled price, a saving—in the case of iron and steel, for example—of perhaps 50 to 65 per cent of the open and black market prices.

Having obtained his site, his machinery, and his materials, the entrepreneur was ready to begin production. Technical problems might arise, however, especially for the man who was new to industry. In that case, The Small Industries Service Institute (SISI) could provide technically trained personnel—chemical engineers, metallurgists, and the like—to help solve problems. If the industrial process was running satisfactorily but the industrialist was having problems with his staff, the SISI provided both management consultancy services and classes in management. The state Small Industries Corporation also provided some technical and managerial assistance. If skilled labor was needed, the Industrial Training Institute could supply it. If the industrialist needed specialized tools or facilities but could not justify the investment, the state would probably provide them: a number of the industrial estates were equipped with common facilities such as hardness-treatment and quality-control centers.

When the goods were completed, the government had programs to assist the small industrialist in marketing and distributing them. First, the government prepared a list of "reserved" items to be purchased by them exclusively from small-scale suppliers (GOI, DCSSI, n.d.b: 622–24). Second, the government offered manufacturers of nonreserved items a price preference of up to 15 per cent above the lowest acceptable bid submitted by a large-scale concern on bids for government orders. Third, the state Small Industries Corporation provided market advice and assistance, and had been experimenting with acting as agents for small industrialists, negotiating for large orders that could then be subcontracted among a number of producers. In some states, the Small Industries Corporation acted as a centralized export clearing-house. At the central government level, the State Trading Corporation (STC), which was the liaison between Indian manufacturers and foreign markets, had likewise experimented with subcontracting bulk orders among producers and with buying all the output from a group of concerns manufacturing the same thing, and offering it in lots for sale abroad. For domestic trade, the NSIC had set up wholesale depots where products were tested for quality, with those meeting standards marked with a brand name (Sundaram, n.d.: 36). Finally, the government offered a roster of miscellaneous facilities and concessions, including subsidies on the purchase of power, tax advantages (including exemption from many taxes and duties for variable time periods for new industries), and, in some states, participation in the cost of feasibility studies. It even provided a special committee to consider needs not anticipated in the formal program.

The Small-Scale Industries Program, then, provided industrialists with a comprehensive, integrated package of assistance measures covering every phase of entrepreneurial activity. The question is, did it work?

Implementation

No program works as well in practice as its version on paper suggests. Officials charged with implementing policy may be uninformed or confused about facilities to be made available and procedures to be followed. Communications and support networks—meant to provide information and materials—may become snarled, preventing effective implementation even when lower-level officials are informed and eager to carry out their mandate. The Small-Scale Industries Program suffered from all of these problems, perhaps the more so because the program itself was so comprehensive and because it required the coordination of so many different agencies at all levels of government.

We will here sketch briefly some of the difficulties of converting the program into practice, reserving for separate treatment some of the more complex problems of implementation. Going back to the career of our hypothetical entrepreneur, let us review some of the areas in which reality falls short of the aspirations of policy.

We begin at the Small Industries Service Institute, where an asppriring entrepreneur trying to decide what kind of industry to set up might have started out. Having looked at the list of titles of the handbooks about the various industries and selected half a dozen of interest, he discovered four of the handbooks were not in stock, and no one knew when new copies would be available. Either new stock had not even been ordered, or the order was placed but returned from the government storage depot marked "not available." The handbooks that were available at the SISI were badly produced. The instructions were sketchy or highly condensed, and the print was hard to read. A more serious problem was the audience at which they seemed to be aimed. Printed in English or Hindi, they outlined the most professionalized, thorough, and expensive route to the production of most items. They urged the manufacturer of a complex tool or machine to make most of the parts himself, which would require a large investment and perhaps also inefficient use of capital, since identical parts could often be bought inexpensively in the market. Most of the plans required a level of capital investment far beyond what most aspirant manufacturers had available, and indeed far beyond the actual investments in most functioning small-scale industries. The aspiring entrepreneur would be discouraged. Perhaps he would look for a job in someone else's industry, or join his brother's company, or stay in his low-level government job.

Alternatively, he might have asked for the technical reports or market forecasts on the industry he had tentatively decided to establish. They were hopelessly out of date. Not realizing this, he might have decided to set up in a field that was already saturated, and find, a year later, that there was no market for his product. One of our respondents, a highly successful and respected manufacturer of precision instruments, had an experience that illustrates this problem all too well. As, among other things, the largest manufacturer of sextants in India, he was troubled by the slack market for this item, and had cut back production. Since he did not want to release his skilled technicians, and since he had the capital to take on a new line, he contacted his local SISI and asked them to supply a list of precision items one might manufacture that had good marketing prospects. In fairly short order, he received the list he had requested. The top-ranked item on the list was—sextants.

Suppose that the entrepreneur had set up a modest manufacturing enterprise turning out trunks and buckets from iron sheets. He had the money to rent a workshop and to buy the hammers and snips and other miscellaneous tools he needed, but he had little money left to buy his raw materials, which were very expensive. Having heard that he could obtain a small loan on his signature, he went to his District Industries Officer to apply. There he learned that such loans are in fact available—but they are to be used only for fixed capital investments, not for working capital. Likewise, neither the State Financial Corporation nor any of the other government agencies established to help the small industrialist gave loans for working capital. The industrialist then had to go to the bank. As we have discussed, however, the banks, even after nationalization, were not enthusiastic about giving loans— particularly very small loans—to small industrialists. Moreover, the industrialist was unable to obtain a loan from the bank simply on his signature; he had to put up tangible security that he was quite unlikely to have. Without working capital, small industrialists cannot upgrade the quality of their goods or compete for large contracts. Yet most of the small industrialists in our Orissa and Tamilnadu samples fell into the category of people too small for help, a pattern, according to the *Report of the Banking Commission* (GOI, 1972), that was replicated over most of India.

Even assuming that an industrialist wanted his loan for fixed investment rather than for working capital, the process of obtaining it was by no means as simple as it sounds. Although the District Industries Officer could grant small loans on his own authority, he was likely to avoid taking that responsibility, preferring to push the application up the official hierarchy, adding to red tape and causing delay. Officials in some states were reluctant to grant unsecured loans at all, fearing that the borrower would default. If that happened, not only would that sum of money be removed permanently from the loan fund pool, but the official who granted the loan was likely to be censured for his bad judgment. At the same time, officials may have been reluctant to make large, safe loans because large loans reduce the number of people who can be helped from a loan fund pool of fixed size. This was made eminently clear to us in Orissa, where we queried the Director of Industries about why he thought it was that we had found, in our interviewing to that point, only one industrialist who had taken a loan from the government. Apparently sharing the quite erroneous official wisdom that most small-scale industrialists—especially those whom two American scholars would choose to interview— are *large* small industrialists, he said:

> Loans from the state are limited to Rs. 50,000 because they come out of consolidated funds. And we are naturally keen not to use these up, especially not to duplicate the functions which can better be provided by the banks. These loans are very desirable, however, because if the loanee does not default, the rate of interest is 4 per cent. This is extremely low, and it is so intentionally, because naturally we are trying to encourage the small industries by every means we can. . . . The point is, you will not be finding people who have taken loans from government because the amounts that government gives are too small. The big firms will not take these loans. That is because the Director of Industries wants to help only the very small people. Naturally you won't be finding these, because they will be only in the villages, not in Cuttack city itself.

In fact, he was wrong on two counts. Over 35 per cent of our Orissa sample had a capital investment of under Rs. 5,000 and nearly half (46.6 per cent) had an investment of less than Rs. 10,000. Of our respondents, most (79 per cent) operated their industries in Cuttack city itself. These kinds of official misunderstandings and bureaucratic conservatisms led in some states to the paradox of small industries unable to get loans while at the same time substantial state loan funds were idle.

Apart from problems of finance, obtaining raw materials was the most enduring dilemma the majority of our respondents faced. We reserve a detailed treatment of this problem for a later chapter. Here, however, we should note that the government saw the provision of controlled-price materials as an integral part of the Small-Scale Industries Program, designed to ensure equitable distribution of scarce resources at fair prices, and hence providing a service to industrialists. Our respondents, by contrast, in general saw government materials control as an imposition that added yet another layer of red tape to their operations, created as many production and management problems as it solved, and complicated even further an already complex raw materials market situation. In the context of official rhetoric about materials control, the number of respondents who simply did not apply to the government for an allocation even though they required controlled materials (51 respondents out of 124 users) and the number who used their allocation as only one among several regular sources of supply, including the black market (61 of 124), are startling. Only 12 of 124 eligible respondents, fewer than 10 per cent, claimed to rely solely on their government allocation for materials supply, and even this number may be inflated by those who wanted to conceal illegal sources.

Of all the types of assistance provided by the Small-Scale Industries Program, the hire-purchase of machinery seemed the most successful. Several of our respondents had bought one or more machines through this program, and they seemed almost unanimously satisfied with the process and its outcome. Of course, the procedures were complicated and time-consuming, especially to buy an imported machine, but small-scale industrialists who used the government program at all were no strangers to red tape.

Again, however, the hire-purchase plan was aimed principally at the large small industrialist rather than at the mass of small producers who constitute the bulk of the small-scale sector. While in principle even a very small manufacturer could use the plan to buy a machine for, say Rs. 500, in practice virtually none did so. The rigors of filling out forms—especially stringent for the illiterate, who must pay a scribe to do it for them; visiting government offices (where one may be turned away if one does not have a calling card that can be brought in to the official one has come to see); and following the progress of the application through correspondence and repeated visits to government offices (which may be time-consuming and costly: a number of our smaller manufacturers said they were obliged to suspend production for a day in order to make such a trip) all discouraged most small producers from applying. Despite an official policy of bringing services to "the grass-roots," the government did little reaching out to small-scale industrialists. Technical assistance in solving problems in the manufacturing process itself was the only service routinely made available at the manufacturer's work site. For the rest, manufacturers had to go to the District Industries Office or the SISI, of which there was generally only one per district. For producers who lived and worked in villages and must walk six miles down dirt roads to reach the nearest main road (and bus service), a trip to see the District Industries Officer was no small undertaking. Like the poor in the United States—who may, for example, lose a day's pay while waiting with a sick child in a clinic for free medical care—the marginal small-scale industrialists in India often forwent the benefits to which they were entitled to avoid incurring the costs associated with them.

When a small-scale industrialist had technical problems, he often could count on prompt assistance from the SISI. Here the difficulty was not lack of response, but its quality. Most of the industrialists we interviewed who had requested technical help complained that the "experts" sent from the SISI often knew less than they themselves did about the nature of the process and the problem. This did not seem to us to be idle grumbling, because two technical experts—one in Tamilnadu, who was a wizard with plating problems, and one in Punjab who was highly knowledgeable about stitching—were singled out repeatedly for praise. The remainder, judging from the stories told about them, richly deserved the contempt in which they were held. Those high-level officials in New Delhi who were willing to take a hard look at how the program was really operating acknowledged a shortage of technical advisers in the field, attributing it to the unanticipated growth in demand that had taken place along with the growth of the small-scale sector. Whatever the cause, however, the lack of trained advisers constituted a real and continuing problem in the implementation of the Small-Scale Industries Program.

Likewise, a manufacturer who had trouble obtaining skilled workers could expect little help from the government's graduates of the Industrial Training Institutes (ITIs). The issue was somewhat complicated, first, because as with many parts of the program, provision of trained workers was really aimed at the larger, technically more sophisticated producers. Many of our industrialists needed, at most, semi-skilled labor to fill positions for which ITI graduates were, in principle, overtrained. Whether from necessity or from a preference for cheap labor, these men almost all trained their own workers, apprenticing them in low-level positions, and instructing them in technical matters on the job. Second, a number of our industrialists ran family enterprises with no outside employees, preferring in some cases to send a son or nephew for technical training to hiring a skilled outsider. Of those concerns that did employ outside labor, many owners preferred to hire workers known to them through family or village networks or through other manufacturers engaged in similar enterprises. Nonetheless, 12 of our respondents did at one time try hiring an ITI graduate on their own, and another 6 did so because the government required firms that employed more than 30 workers to hire one ITI graduate for each 30 workers employed. Their responses to these workers were almost unanimously negative, with complaints ranging from bad work habits to lack of knowledge about how to perform the job for which they had supposedly been trained. Clearly, small-scale industrialists who had labor shortage problems did not, with some justification, look on the ITIs as a resource for solving them. Further, it was not all clear that shortages of skilled labor was a general problem in the small-scale sector.

Finally, an entrepreneur who had set up a small industry with the hope of obtaining assistance from the government when the time came to market his product would almost certainly have been disappointed. An inspection of the list of 166 "Items Reserved for Purchases from the Small-Scale Sector" in 1971, for example, reveals a rather high level of overlap among the particular items included. Items like Belt Leather, Belt Leather and Strips, Boots and Shoes of all types, Boxing Boots, Brief Cases, Chappals and Sandals, Dust Shield—Leather, Football Boots, Hide and Country Leather, Leather of all types, Laces—Leather, Leather Bags, Leather Boxes, Leather Harness, Sheep Skin—all types, Ski Boots and Shoes, Sole Leather, Spiked Boots, Suitcases, Tip Boots, and Washers—Leather (GOI, DCSSI, n.d.b: 622–24) all sound suspiciously similar, and indeed all of our respondents in leather work had at one time or another made most of these items. Of the remaining marketing programs proposed by the government, most were still in development and testing stages at the time of our study. None of our respondents, so far as we know, had marketed his product through either his state Small Industries Corporation or the NSIC.

Respondents did know about and mention with enthusiasm the 15 per cent price preference for small industries bidding on government orders, but since one was required to manufacture a product that the government bought, be registered with the NSIC, submit tenders (bids for jobs), and be a big enough producer to supply the entire order if one won the contract, many of our industrialists considered themselves ineligible for this benefit.

The imminent entrance of the central government's State Trading Corporation (STC) onto the small-scale scene was regarded with dread by those respondents who knew about the history of STC's operations. These had had mixed success at best, at least in part because of the rapid growth and bloated size of the organization and the wide range of activities it undertook.

Some high government officials, especially those who have spent a large part of their careers in planning and policymaking, take a kind of Olympian view of problems in implementation. One such official, Development Commissioner Small-Scale Industries at the time of our study, remarked in an essay on the strengths of the Small-Scale Industries Program, "It is true that assistance intended to be provided under the programme has not reached the small industrialists always in time and in full measure. Instances of delays and difficulties have also been very common. *But these have been mainly shortcomings in the implementation of the programme, rather than of the programme itself.*" (Alexander, n.d.: 40; our emphasis), as if the value of the program could be assessed by reference to its comprehensiveness and internal elegance rather than by appraising its success in achieving stated goals. At the risk of seeming to belabor the obvious, our view is that effective implementation is a crucial test of a program, and failures of implementation therefore cannot be brushed aside as mere "practical problems." Many beautifully formulated programs have foundered in the transformation from paper to practice.

CHAPTER THREE

THE SMALL-SCALE INDUSTRIES PROGRAM: ADMINISTRATIVE STRUCTURE

In 1975, the Small-Scale Industries Program was administered by a complex, loosely-structured network of central and state government agencies. We have already mentioned many of these agencies, but let us here look more systematically at what they were, what they did, and how they related to one another.

Administration at the Center

Central government organizations were in principle charged primarily with policy and program formulation. Implementation was a secondary responsibility, and then only in areas of all-India concern or where adequate resources were not available in the states. The bulk of the responsibility for implementation thus rested with the individual states (Roy, n.d.: 28). They in turn interpreted and carried out the policy directives emanating from the center in a variety of ways, giving each state's version of the program a somewhat different flavor from that of the others.

At the head of the program were two central government agencies: the Small-Scale Industries Board and the Central Small Industries Organization (CSIO), also known as the Small-Scale Industries Development Organisation (SSIDO). The Small-Scale Industries Board was purely a policymaking body, charged with overall responsibility for planning and coordinating the development of small-scale industries. It had no implementing functions, and no agencies responsible to it that might carry out its recommendations. Rather, the Board passed its suggestions directly to the Industries Ministry for incorporation into formal government policy. The CSIO, by contrast, although in principle also an advisory and coordinating agency which acted as a liaison between state governments and other central government agencies, was in fact the top-level executive agency of the program as well. Its functions included the establishment and supervision of lower-level agencies located in the states but accountable to the CSIO at the center (i.e., they were formally a part of the central government administrative structure, not the state government structure), and educational and publicity activities ranging from the preparation of technical handbooks and publicity brochures to the conduct of small-scale industries fairs.

The Small-Scale Industries Board, created in November 1954, comprised central and state government officials (exofficio), including the (central government) Minister for Industries, a development officer from the CSIO, and Directors of Industries from the state Departments of Industries; representatives of selected central and state level public sector corporations such as the National Small Industries Corporation and the state Financial Corporations; representatives of financial institutions such as the Reserve Bank of india, the State Bank of India, and other banks; officers of the Federation of Small-Scale Industries Associations; and various non-official trade, industry, and other representatives constituting a total membership by 1966 of 59 persons (GOI, DCSSI, n.d.a: 59, 231).

Activities of the Board have included recommendations establishing the basic outlines of the Small-Scale Industries Program (such as formulating the definition of a small-scale unit, requesting the state governments to establish industrial estates and programs for supplying machinery on hire-purchase, and encouraging state electricity boards to reduce the tariff on power for small-scale units [Meeting of January 1955]; establishing purchase and payment guidelines for the National Small Industries Corporation (Meeting of August 1955); recommending that the states liberalize their rules for granting loans to small industrialists, and recommending the preparation and supply, to the state Directors of Industries, of model plans for setting up small-scale units (Meeting of December 1955); and encouraging the NSIC to discuss programs with the Director General, Supplies and Disposals, for the reservation of items to be manufactured by and purchased from small industries (Meeting of March 1956) (GOI, DCSSI, n.d.a: 231–38). That most of the recommendations were later implemented as part of the Small-

Scale Industries Program testifies to the seriousness with which the Board's advisory role was treated by the government.

The Central Small Industries Organization was an office of the central government, but one that was outside the "line" organization consisting of ministries headed by elected ministers who set policy, and civil servant secretaries to government who were accountable to the minister for implementation. The Development Commissioner Small-Scale Industries (DCSSI) is a top-level position approximately equivalent in rank to that of a secretary. Unlike a secretary, however—who has through frequent transfers spent some portion of his career in virtually every state-level department of government (see Taub, 1969: 29–59)—the DCSSI may have spent most of the later part of his career at various levels within the small-scale industries organization itself.

The CSIO was structured administratively much like a central government ministry or a department of state government. The Development Commissioner supervised a staff of subordinates, each of whom was responsible for an area such as chemical industries, industrial estates, economic investigation and statistics, and industrial management and training. One director sat in addition as Secretary of the Small-Scale Industries Board (GOI, DCSSI, n.d.a: 59).

The CSIO had several important functions in addition to coordination, education, and publicity. First, it established and maintained Small Industries Service Institutes throughout India. The SISIs were located in the states, but were arms of the central government, accountable to the CSIO rather than to the state Departments of Industries. In 1968, there were more than eighty SISIs and Industrial Extension Centres throughout the country (Roy, n.d.: 29), charged, as we have outlined in discussing the program, with providing advice on industry setup and site selection, marketing reports, technical assistance, and management training courses for small-scale industrialists.

Second, the CSIO had the responsibility of representing the small-scale sector as a whole to many of the various agencies responsible for allocating raw materials. The CSIO distributed priority guidelines to the states to be used in allocating materials to industry. The state in turn prepared and submitted its raw materials requests to the CSIO, which passed them on to the appropriate allocating agencies. When overall allocations for each sector (small-scale, medium-scale and large-scale) had been made, the CSIO apportioned the small-scale sector's share among the states.

Likewise, the CSIO maintained a close relationship with the State Trading Corporation and the Minerals and Metals Trading Corporation (MMTC) to channel ("canalize") a share of imported raw materials to the small-scale sector (GOI, DCSSI, n.d.a: 133–45); Nanjappa, n.d.: vi).

Finally, the CSIO protected the interests of the small-scale sector before the Licensing Committee, which reviewed applications to establish larger-scale enterprises, by speaking against the licensing of prospective units likely to be competitive with existing units in the small-scale sector (Nanjappa, n.d.: vi).

The small Industries Extension Training Institute, an autonomous central government organization located in Hyderabad, offered courses in industrial management and "area development." The former were intended principally for government officers at various levels in the Small Industries Organization, to equip them in management counseling and hence improve the quality of managerial advisory services they were able to provide to indusrialists. The latter were aimed mainly at District Industries Officers in the state governments, to teach them both some development economics and some techniques for assessing an area's industrial development potential (GOI, DCSSI, n.d.a: 209–10).

Occupying a somewhat lower rank than the Small-Scale Industries Board and the CSIO in the status hierarchy of central government agencies was the National Small Industries Corporation, a semi-autonomous public-sector (government-owned) organization created in 1955 to link the purchasing power of the Government of India with the products and requirements of the small-scale sector. The NSIC's responsibilities were almost completely implementative, as we shall see below. First, however, let us discuss briefly what a government corporation is and how it relates to the formal government administrative structure.

Beginning in the mid-1950s, both the central and state governments began to establish separate, incorporated agencies to deal with certain areas that had previously come wholly under the jurisdiction of departments (or ministries) in the regular administrative hierarchy. These corporations are semi-autonomous in the sense that they are created by and accountable to the government, which names the Managing Director and some members of the Board of Directors, but at the same time, the corporations are not bound by many of the rules defining decisionmaking procedures within the administrative structure. In establishing such organizations, the government hoped to take advantage of the greater flexibility and responsiveness to changing conditions that are more characteristic of private enterprise than of government bureaucracy. Also, by establishing such organizations outside of the civil service hierarchy, the government would be able to recruit technically qualified and experienced non-government personnel to staff them. Career government servants can and do serve in them without losing seniority, but in principle only to fill gaps caused by the unavailability of private sector managerial talent. Until 1972, they could do so only on loan from the government administrative service to which they were formally attached. In 1972, the government began attempting to require civil servants to choose either a career of regular administrative service or a career in the government corporations.

In practice, these corporations have had a mixed record. Some—notably the State Trading Corporation—became as characterized by elaborate rules and red tape as the official departments they were meant to sidestep. In contrast, some provided a means that would otherwise have been unavailable for making the talents of private sector personnel available to the government.

The earliest of the National Small Industries Corporation assistance programs was the Government Stores Purchase Program, which secured orders from the Director General, Supplies and Disposals (DGS&D) to be filled by small producers. Small-scale units had to register with the NSIC for participation in the program, but registration entitled them to benefits, such as free forms for submitting bids; exemption, on certification of competency by NSIC, from payment of security deposits on jobs; price preference up to 15 per cent over the lowest acceptable bid submitted by a larger-scale unit; and, in case of rejection of bids, grievance and redress facilities from DGS&D via the NSIC. Small industries that won DGS&D contracts could arrange generous financing toward the completion of the job from the State Bank of India through the NSIC, which guaranteed the loan. The NSIC was, further, responsible for extending the list of items to be purchased by the DGS&D exclusively from the small-scale sector (Sundaram, n.d.:|32–34).

The NSIC's other major program, discussed earlier, was the hire-purchase plan for small industrialists who wanted to buy machinery. The NSIC also had marketing assistance programs, but these had been less successful by 1975 than the government purchase and hire-purchase programs. The NSIC also operated Prototype Production and Training Centers, established both to design and test new products that could be manufactured in the small-scale sector and to train workers and managerial personnel (Sundaram, n.d.: 34–37). These centers were more costly and less effective than NSIC had hoped.

Administration in the States

In a State, the Department of Industries, through its Directorate of Industries, played a coordinating and implementing role analogous to that of the Central Small Industries Organization. The state Small-Scale Industries Board, a counterpart to the Small-Scale Industries Board at the center, advised the Industries Department in the formulation of policy; but since the broad outlines of policy are established at the center, the policymaking functions of the Department of Industries were rather circumscribed, and the role of the state Small Industries Board was correspondingly limited.

Typically, the Directorate of Industries was responsible for developing industrial estates, including developing land and providing sheds and common facilities; allocating raw materials; offering loans under the State Aid to Industries Act (1951); certifying import requirements; organizing training and model production programs; and establishing industrial cooperatives. The Director of Industries was supervised by an under-secretary for industries, a joint or deputy secretary for industries, and, at the head of the department, the Secretary for Industries. The Director was, however, the highest-ranking officer directly concerned with the operation of the Small-Scale Industries Program. To him also fell many of the liaison functions that connected small industrialists with the programs that emanated from the center.

Below the Director were Additional Directors or Joint Directors of Industry, one of whom might be responsible for industrial estates, one for rural industries, one for administration, and one for small-scale industries. The Additional (or Joint) Director for Small-Scale Industries, in turn, supervised a staff of Deputy Directors, one of whom oversaw engineering, another handicrafts, another chemicals, another leather, and so on. There were also several regional Joint and Deputy Directors, each of whom was responsible for supervising the operations of perhaps three or four District Industries Officers (GOI, DCSSI, n.d.a: 207). The District Industries Officer (DIO) was ordinarily the highest-ranking officer to deal directly with the public. In general, applications for loans, raw materials, essentiality certificates for imported machinery, and the like were submitted to his office and passed to the appropriate level or agency of government for consideration. The Department of Industries was flanked by several government corporations having specialized responsibilities in implementing of the Small-Scale Industries Program. The state Small Industries Corporation, parallel (not subordinate) to the National Small Industries Corporation, generally executed the distribution of raw materials, ran a program for hire-purchase of machinery, processed government orders for products and subcontracted them to small units, and sometimes provided limited financial, technical, and managerial help. Some states had a Small Industries Development Corporation rather than a Small Industries Corporation, but the functions were broadly the same.

The state Financial Corporation was strictly a funding agency, serving industries at all size levels. In general, it made fixed capital loans whose minimum size was at or just below the maximum offered by the state through the Department of Industries, and whose maximum was Rs. 2 million to Rs. 2.5 million. Financial Corporations were permitted under special circumstances (such as to keep a loan recipient in business) to give working capital loans as well. Financial Corporation loans were always at subsidized rates, although the interest level, loan minima and maxima, and repayment provisions varied somewhat from state to state.

The preceding description is a model of the typical small industries administrative arrangement within a state as seen in 1975, but as with any model, the actual structure in each state departed from it. Of the three states we studied, Punjab most closely fit the model. The Small Industries Corporation, however, had more extensive responsibilities. One section handled small industry exports such as of machine tools, and another managed a state-owned hosiery (knitted goods) factory. The Punjab Small Industries Corporation also managed the state government emporia, which in most states are retail outlets for the handicrafts produced there. In Punjab, however, the government emporia also sold the products of small-scale industry. A visitor to such a shop might be jolted a bit when he first noticed, between the shelves of hand-embroidered silk blouses and etched brass cigarette boxes, a row of shiny toasters gleaming invitingly.

In addition to the Small Industries Corporation and the Financial Corporation, Punjab had an Industrial Development Corporation. Since Punjab had an enormous number of small-scale industries—nearly 27,000 registered units in 1975, and 65,445 in 1982—and a minuscule number of large enterprises (Managing Director, Punjab IDC, personal communication), the main concern of the Industrial Development Corporation there was to stimulate the growth of larger-scale industry in the state. In partnership with the government, it established several larger-scale enterprises which, however, affected the small-scale sector as well, creating the opportunity for ancillary industries to supply them with parts.

Tamilnadu presented some different variations on the theme. In addition to the Small Industries Development Corporation (SIDCO), which carried out the functions of the small industries corporation as described above, it also had a second small industries corporation, the Tamilnadu Small Industries Corporation (TANSI), whose responsibility was to manage some 60 government-owned small-scale firms. These firms were established both as demonstration projects to show the people of Tamilnadu what could be done in the small-scale field and as a means for distributing industries—and hence also employment—throughout the state. Although they served all of these purposes to some extent, many of these small industries were not economically competitive, and from time to time the worst moneylosers were shut down. The government faced a dilemma here, because these industries employed many thousands of workers. If profitability were the sole criterion used to assess them, many more would have had to be closed; but this would have led to a massive increase in unemployment.

By historical accident, Tamilnadu had no Financial Corporation, but rather had an Industrial Investment Corporation that increasingly took on the responsibilities held by financial corporations in other states. The Industrial Investment Corporation was set up as a company in 1949, and hence has a different internal structure and is subject to different regulations from those of the ordinary government corporation. When the State Financial Corporations Act (1951) was passed, the Industrial Investment Corporation was allowed to stand in place of a financial corporation, while keeping its original structure under company law. It came under pressure from the government, however, to act more like other state financial corporations and provide more help to small industrialists. As a result, between 1969 and the end of 1971, the amount of the minimum loan to be granted by the IIC was reduced, first from Rs. 200,000 to Rs. 100,000, then to Rs. 50,000 and finally to Rs. 25,000. The management of the IIC was rather unhappy about this development. Their workload had increased substantially, especially since, as the secretary to the organization told us, "We must carry out the same investigations for a loan of Rs. 25,000 to a small-scale industry as we do for a loan of 2.5 lakhs [Rs. 250,000] for a medium- or large-scale industry."

Consonant with the underdeveloped condition of small industries in Orissa was an atrophied small industries administrative structure. While Orissa did have a Financial Corporation, it had no Small Industries Corporation. One had been established in the early 1960s, with the intent of helping in the procurement and storage of raw materials and also to provide marketing assistance to small industrialists. According to a high Orissa official, the Corporation "did little of the first and none of the second." Consequently, in 1968 it turned its energy to agroindustries, getting agricultural machinery to the villages, making it work, and keeping it running. As a result, the Directorate of Industries in Orissa performed all the functions usually handled by small industries corporations in other states, as well as the usual activities of the Directorate. Because of the low level of small-industrial activity in Orissa, however, this added responsibility did not seem to place an undue strain on the facilities of the Directorate.

Consequences

We see, then, that the formal allocation of policymaking responsibilities to the center and implementation responsibilities to the states was not so clearly drawn in practice. It is true that policy planning and coordination was done principally at the center, with the states more likely determining the emphases to be given to the various parts of the program than shaping the program itself. At the same time, however, the center took responsibility for implementing some parts of the program, and not merely those for which the states could not supply the resources. Some services, such as the technical advice and assistance provided by the SISIs, could as easily be supplied by the states; but because they were initially provided by the central government, they were likely, through the process by which existing institutions become permanent, to continue to be so.

Sometimes the center acted in concert with or even duplicated the functions of state agencies. For example, the Haryana Small Industries Corporation hire-purchase program was operated independently of the National Small Industries Corporation, with the state corporation placing orders and buying directly from manufacturers. Other states' small industries corporations acted as central agents for the state industrialists, collecting and pooling machinery orders to send on to the NSIC; and, under the Government Stores Purchase program, receiving large contracts for products from the NSIC which they then subcontracted to local industrialists. In still other states, such as Orissa, which had no small industries corporation, direct application to the NSIC (through the state Directorate of Industries) was the only access that local industrialists had to these parts of the Small-Scale Industries Program.

Clearly, the administrative structure of the Small-Scale Industries Program was elaborate. Although a planner or a scholar might readily understand the formal allocations of responsibility among these agencies, it was a good deal more difficult for an ordinary user of the program to do so. Several respondents reported traipsing all over town, from one government office to another, before finding the one that was authorized to give the kind of assistance they required. Many industrialists found the sheer number of different agencies, all part of the program, confusing. When we asked, for example, whether they had applied for their loans to the Department of Industries or to the state Financial Corporation, they were apt to reply, "I don't know. I just applied to 'the small industries'." Sophisticated respondents expressed despair at the decentralization of responsibilities, and the consequent multiplication of visits to offices, forms to fill out, and the like. One respondent in Tamilnadu, when asked if there were additional services he thought the government should provide, said:

> Well, I mean to say that they don't have to create any *new* departments. Plenty of departments are there now. . . . The point really is, that if they fulfilled all of the existing programs which they have already, they would do very well. Now there are just too many departments and too much red tape. If we make some application, we have to march from one office to another. I don't have time to do that. I say, let them have one public relations office only. Let them have some package system whereby you have a form to fill up—and they can ask whatever questions they want. They can make you fill up one hundred copies of the form; that is all right. But then let them take your application form, and send it to the first department. When that department sanctions, let *them* send a letter to the State Bank saying this man has been sanctioned for a loan for thus and such an amount. Let *them* send it to the department which is responsible for giving licenses, saying this man has been sanctioned for a license for

thus and such an amount. As it is now, we ourselves must go to each of these places. Let them eliminate our trips to Delhi and Calcutta. . . . Again, it is not that the programs are not there, or that they are not good in their idea. The trouble is that there is so much of wastage. I should say that of all the funds allocated for these various projects, about 75 per cent is utilized in administering the programs and only 25 per cent is going for helping the people who are supposed to be helped.

A number of respondents, faced with the complexities of dealing with the number of offices relevant to their problem, preferred to attack the problem without help from the government. Clearly, then, the administrative structure itself is a source of problems in the implementation of the Small-Scale Industries Program.

Conclusion

We have seen that although the Small-Scale Industries Program was an extraordinarily comprehensive program of assistance to entrepreneurs, problems of achieving maximum benefits from it arose from several sources. First, the government was trying to increase small industry activity at too many levels. Equal emphasis was placed on increasing the number of industrial units and raising the output of existing concerns. In the face of an acute raw materials shortage, it was impossible to achieve these objectives simultaneously. Administrators in Tamilnadu were beginning to realize this at the time of the study and were moving to limit the number of industries eligible for official raw materials allocations.

Second, the program was plagued with too many goals, some of which conflicted. The government hoped to alleviate, in a single stroke, shortages of consumer goods, capital, and management. It sought to reduce both urban and rural unemployment, increasing opportunity for skilled engineers and unskilled labor alike. The program was meant to reduce concentrations of economic power and equalize the condition of all citizens. Industry was to be dispersed into the countryside, benefiting the rural poor both economically and socially while increasing national output.

Because these multiple aims conflicted, resources were wasted in scattershot investment in a broad range of undertakings. These resources might have yielded better returns had they been intensively concentrated on those undertakings most likely to produce large gains rapidly. The initial high-yield efforts would have generated additional capital that could be directed toward lower-yield projects and those requiring longer gestation.

Third, officials were confused about who their clients were, imagining the majority of small-scale industrialists to be large and rich, whereas in reality they were small and poor. This misperception led to confusing rhetoric about reaching down the social ladder to recruit new industrialists and help existing ones, when in fact the majority of the programs—either because of the sophisticated problems they were there to solve, or because of the costs incurred by the industrialist in participating—could be effectively used only by a relatively affluent minority of the potential client pool. In this context, it is astonishing that a package of incentives and services as exhaustive as the Small-Scale Industries Program made no provision for supplying small amounts of working capital. This is the only type of assistance that would have benefited the majority of our respondents.

Finally, effective administration of the program was hindered by the multiplicity of services provided. Coordinating the numerous agencies inherently produced delay and inefficiency even where officials were individually hardworking, energetic, and eager to perform well. Teaching clients to function effectively in such a milieu is especially difficult. A certain number who could have benefited from the programs did not use them because they did not understand how to fit themselves into the system.

CHAPTER FOUR

THE STUDY

The concentrations of small-scale industry in India vary in density enormously from state to state. In 1975, Punjab led the remaining states (except Delhi, which is not directly comparable) by a margin of more than three to one. Punjab had one registered small-scale unit for every 528 people. Maharashtra, next in rank, had one per 1,957. Punjab's figure is striking even if one assumes that the proportion of fraudulent industries is higher there than in other states. At the bottom of the scale stood Himachal Pradesh, tucked away in the northern mountains, with just 93 small-scale units, or one for every 37,204 people.

Between these extremes, the remaining states clustered roughly into high and low groups. Included in the high cluster were Gujarat, with one registered small-scale industry for every 2,082 people; Tamilnadu, at one per 2,571; and West Bengal, with one per 2,951. This list ranged down fairly evenly through six more states to Jammu and Kashmir, with one industry for every 4,859 people there. Then a sharp break occurred. Orissa was next, with one per 7,778 people, followed by Haryana, Assam, Bihar, and Himachal Pradesh. (Figures were computed from GOI, DCSSI, n.d.b: 721 and GOI, 1971a.) With the exception of Haryana, this low group ranked at the bottom of the Indian states on most socioeconomic indicators. Haryana was low in small-scale industries in part because it was high in large-scale ones. The reverse was in some measure true for Punjab. That is, Punjab did have very few larger-scale industries; but this alone does not account for all the difference in small industry concentration between Punjab and the other states. The situations of Haryana and Punjab were in part an artifact of their creation from the portion of the old state of East Punjab. The industrial picture in the original East Punjab was more balanced.

Selecting the States

In selecting the states to include in our study, we thought it important to have a range of industrial concentration; and, because of cultural differences between north and south India, to have geographical diversity as well. Clearly, we had to include Punjab; and it was easy to select Orissa, on the east coast, to represent the low group, because we had lived there from 1962 to 1964 and were familiar with the state. The choice of a middle-level state was difficult. Originally, we had hoped to study West Bengal. Calcutta, its major city, is with Bombay one of India's two most important industrial centers. Small-scale industries have been an important part of Calcutta's economic life for a long time, and many do very high quality work. Our guess was that West Bengal had more small-scale industries per person than Tamilnadu, our ultimate choice, although offical figures suggested otherwise. West Bengal had been maladministered for so long that its small industries were probably markedly underregistered. (A survey conducted by the Ford Foundation in West Bengal in 1964 had found 308,000 workers, or one-third of the industrial labor force there, in small industries [Ford Foundation, CMPO, 1966].) If we had been able to study West Bengal, we would have had a problem finding a low-density state and still satisfying the geographical criterion. All of the low-density states except Haryana are in the northeast quadrant of India; and Haryana is adjacent to Punjab. In any case, we were unable because of chaotic political conditions to obtain permission to study West Bengal.

Tamilnadu, we knew, had experienced dramatic growth in the small-scale sector in the decade between the mid-1960s and the mid-1970s. Since we were interested in exploring the relationship between the Small-Scale Industries Program and growth in the small-scale sector, the increase attracted our attention, especially because expansion began just when the full program shifted into high gear. In addition, we had more personal acquaintances in Tamilnadu and more first-hand knowledge of it than of any other southern state. In India, "knowing someone" often makes the difference between accomplishing what one wants to do—be it conducting a research project or getting a telephone installed—and not. The combination, then, of Tamilnadu's growth in the small-scale sector with the promise of somewhat easier access there than in other states led us to select Tamilnadu as our third state.

The Sample Respondents

Because we were interested in both small-scale industrialists and the programs to aid them, we sought two classes of respondents. The first included government officials in each state who were responsible for the small-scale industries program. These always included the Director of Industries and an assistant who was responsible directly for small industries; the Director of the Small Industries Service Institute; and the heads of other public sector agencies—small industries development corporations, industrial development corporations, and financial corporations—responsible for the welfare of small-scale industrialists. We asked these respondents about the dimensions of their programs, the scope of small-scale industries within the state, their biggest problems, and their aspirations. We also sought clarification on complex procedures.

In the three chosen states, we talked to samples of small-scale industrialists. To choose these samples, we were obliged to rely on the compilations of registered industries published by departments of industries in each of the states. As lists representing populations of small-scale industries, these directories had a number of drawbacks, some of which were clearly sources of bias. To begin with, all of the directories were out of date. Revisions had been undertaken at unpredictable intervals, and updating entries was timeconsuming. Consequently, none of the directories was less than two years old according to publication date, so some of the data in them—as well as the lacunae—were older than that. Moreover, the directories were not contemporaneous. Orissa's dated from 1967, Punjab's was prepared in 1965, and Tamilnadu's came in two volumes, the first compiled in 1965, and the second containing additions (but not deletions) through 1969.

The industries included in each of the directories were listed according to type. Unfortunately, the criteria used to categorize the enterprises were not applied consistently. In some cases, the raw materials used determined the category; in others, the end product did. Thus, for example, some manufacturers of plastic items were included under "Plastic and Polythene Products," while others were to be found under "Fountain Pen and Other Writing Materials." Parts manufacturers were sometimes classified by the part itself and sometimes by the larger product for which the part was designed. A manufacturer of spare parts for earthmoving equipment, for example, was listed under "Trailers, Harvesters, the Like, and Their Spares," while the manufacturer of another kind of part for similar kinds of machinery was classified under "Ball, Roller, and Tapered Bearings." Occasionally, the same company was listed separately in two or more places.

Further, since the government definition of a small-scale industry put no restrictions on the type of ownership of the industry, the directories included government-owned and cooperatively-owned enterprises in addition to the privately-owned concerns in which we were interested. We included only the latter in our sample.

Occasionally, we would go out to interview a member of our sample only to discover that the chosen enterprise was not a small-scale firm at all. This happened twice in Orissa and twice in Tamilnadu. One of the Tamilnadu industries had originally been a large small-scale unit, and had only recently changed its status to medium-scale. The time lag between revisions of the directory accounted for the error. The other larger-scale enterprise in Tamilnadu, and both in Orissa, however, were astonished to discover that they had been listed as small-scale. The Tamilnadu firm was a branch of a large lubricating-oil company. One of the Orissa companies was part of a Calcutta firm with ten branches; a firm, moreover, that was not manufacturing but only supplying trucks, motorscooters, and other motorized vehicles. The other was a huge enterprise manufacturing sanitary bathroom fittings for distribution all over India.

The most important shortcoming of all these lists was that they included only small-scale industries that were registered with the government. We have already discussed how little is known about unregistered industries, even to what proportion of the small-scale sector they represent. Unfortunately, our study does little to illuminate this area. Ideally, we would have liked to take area censuses in each of our three sample locations to learn something about unregistered industries as well as registered ones. Because of time limitations, this was impossible. The one fairly safe guess we can make about unregistered industries as a group is that they fall at the low end of all factory dimensions: size, output, level of mechanization, number of employees, and gross income.

Virtually all industries beyond the subsistence level register because they need something from the government, be it raw materials, technical assistance, funds for expansion, import licenses, contracts for their product, or whatever. Moreover, the larger enterprises are visible: they must pay taxes and keep records, and they can anticipate a visit from government inspectors at any time, checking on working conditions, the legal status of employees, or the condition of the books. Being in the eye of the government means, among other things, that one may be asked to register even if one has not taken anything from it. Hence, while it is conceivable that a prosperous industry is unregistered because it has neither had dealings with the government nor come to its attention, it is quite unlikely that many such enterprises exist. We are therefore fairly certain that our lists were systematically biased toward the larger, more affluent, more technologically sophisticated, "modern" industries—that is, toward the type of industry at which the Small-Scale Industries Program is really aimed. It will be important to bear this bias in mind when we turn to the analysis of our data.

Sampling Procedures

Armed with our directories, we turned to drawing our sample. The directories were all organized by districts (roughly equivalent to counties) within the state. In the interest of economy, while recognizing that this would further bias our sample, we decided, for each state, to let the district with the most small-scale industries represent the state. It was from these most industrially populous districts that we drew our samples.

Not surprisingly, these industrial districts were also densely populated with humans. In Orissa, we chose Cuttack District, which includes Cuttack city, the largest in the state, with a population of some 300,000 in 1971. Also in Cuttack District is Kendrapara, a large town 90 miles northeast of Cuttack city. In Tamilnadu, we chose Madras District, of which Madras city, a city of 2.5 million people, constitutes virtually the entirety. In Punjab, we initially selected Ludhiana District, but for reasons we will outline shortly, decided to add adjacent Jullundur District. These two districts included, respectively, Ludhiana city (population 400,000) and Jullundur city (population 200,000). Although neither Ludhiana nor Jullundur was a very large city, the state of Punjab (and, indeed, the region comprising Punjab, Haryana, and Delhi) is something of a megalopolis. In Punjab, industry and agriculture—the most modern in India—are fairly evenly dispersed. Unlike Orissa, where one sets out on a long car journey with a hamper of food (enough to last several days, in case of breakdown) and a car trunk full of tools and spare parts, there are very few isolated rural areas ("mofussil areas," as the local people call them) in Punjab. Consequently, our interviewing sites ranged in the three states from Cuttack District, characterized by towns widely separated by stretches of rural village, through Ludhiana and Jullundur Districts, with their more uniformly dispersed populations, to Madras District, one of the most densely populated, highly urbanized locales in India.

For each of three states, we drew a systematic stratified sample of industries. The directories all arranged the industries into categories (whose limitations we discussed above), so beginning with a randomly generated number, we drew every *n*th name (*n* varied by state) from each state's list, selecting the next industry if the first one chosen was a government- or cooperatively-owned enterprise. We then went back and sampled randomly one name from each category that had been skipped over entirely in the systematic sample. Later, we used the systematic sample to replace out-of-business and unlocatable industries, as well as our two refusals, selecting each successive name until we ran out of entries in a given category.

The Orissa directory listed 425 small-scale industries in Cuttack District, which, when we eliminated multiple entries (18), cooperative societies (20), and government-owned industries (6), was reduced to 381. Consequently, the 12.5 per cent sample we had intended to draw, which yielded 53 names plus 3 additional from skipped categories, was actually about a 14 per cent sample.

After working with the Orissa directory, which encompassed in one slim volume all the registered industries—small-, medium-, and large-scale—in the state, we were startled by the Tamilnadu directory. With only a little more than twice the population of Orissa, Tamilnadu had so many registered small industries alone that two fat tomes were required to list them. In all, 2,944 industries were entered for Madras District. We drew a 2 per cent sample consisting of 58 industries, and supplemented it with an additional 25 names from skipped categories, for a total sample of just under 3 per cent.

For Punjab, we began by selecting a 2 per cent sample of the 2,741 industries in Ludhiana. Before long, it became clear that if we followed this procedure, knitting mills would make up over half of our sample (more than 1,600 of the 2,741 small industries in Ludhiana are knitting mills). We therefore decided on a somewhat more complex sampling strategy. First, to increase the range of industries that could be covered in our Punjab survey, we added Jullundur district to Ludhiana district for our sampling frame

Jullundur has virtually no knitting mills, but has concentrations of several other industries such as the manufacture of athletic equipment. This meant adding 1,832 industries to our original 2,741, for a total of 4,573. From these, we selected an initial sample of 1 per cent, or 45. To this, we added 9 industries sampled from skipped categories. Finally, because Punjab is famous for its machining industries and because we felt that selecting these industries on a 1 per cent basis might exclude some important aspects of the small-scale picture in that state, we raised only the sample of machining industries to 4 per cent, adding 22 new names to our sample, for a total of 76, or about 1.7 per cent.

We have gone into some detail about our sampling procedures to convey what our samples does and does not include and to clarify why we rely on certain kinds of analyses of our data to the exclusion of others.

For many reasons—the exclusion of unregistered industries; the non-comparability of time periods covered by the lists; the small size and peculiar character of our Punjab sample; the use of one or two districts to stand for the whole state; and our inability to locate some of our sampled respondents or, in some cases, to be sure that the respondent located was actually the same one as had appeared in the directory—we do not assume a very close fit between our samples and the populations of small-scale industries in each state. Consequently, we will not attempt to make rigorous statistical inferences from our samples to the true populations.

At the same time, we have a good representation of the dimensions over which small-scale industries vary in the three states. Even bearing in mind the limitations of our samples, this enables us to make some limited, but nonetheless legitimate and useful, kinds of inferences from our samples to the populations.

In 1975, we returned to India to look again at small industries. In the intervening three years, India, along with most of the rest of the world, had gone through a major recession and, in addition, had recently undergone a change in government form. Prime Minister Indira Gandhi had declared the nation to be in a "state of emergency" and abrogated many civil rights. Some of her policies were designed to have a clear impact on business: the right to strike had been abolished, for example, and the government had begun a vigorous program to discourage black marketeering and to locate black money. To assess the impact of these changes and, in addition, to get a longer-term perspective on our industries, we set out to reinterview the more prosperous half of our sample. The more prosperous, we reasoned, would probably still be in business and, consequently, would be easier to find; because of time constraints, we had to reduce sample size and this was a convenient way to do so. We asked each respondent only eight or nine questions. We asked them how business was and tried to get concrete numbers to measure gross revenue and investment. We asked about the availability of raw materials, which had been a problem earlier, checked to see what changes they had made, and tried to see how far they had moved toward realizing their plans.

The Interviews

Our knowledge about administrative procedures and practices arises not only from our formal research but also many informal activities. We sought out people connected with the small industries programs and tried to meet people involved in industry in other ways. These included officials in the small-scale industries program in Delhi and Haryana as well as the Commissioner of Small-Scale Industries for India. Because of our previous research activities, we had numerous acquaintances who served as government officials or spent time in departments of industry. We stalked industrialists at parties and on trains; many of our new acquaintances and friends brought others to meet us. Consequently, when we use explicit numbers, we are drawing them either from our samples or are quoting official statistics, which we identify as such; but when we provide detailed accounts of procedures, practices, or attitudes we may be using information gathered from our extensive informal contacts. In sum, the range of our knowledge about small industries extends far beyond what we learned from our sample. Our sample respondents provided us with an information base to which additional information was added.

The Questionnaire

We conducted our interviews with respondents from sampled industries using a standardized 114-item questionnaire (see the Appendix) that included questions ranging from the respondent's personal history through his work history; the history of the sampled industry; details about other industries owned by the respondent; contacts with the government pertinent to the sampled industry; knowledge about, attitudes toward, and use of the Small-Scale Industries Program; general attitudes toward the government; and concluded with a set of questions attempting to get at the respondent's value orientations. With the exception of the objective questions (e.g., age, years married, original capital investment in the industry) and the values questions, which offered multiple choice responses to a set of statements, the questions were open-ended. Interviews lasted from one to two hours or from two to four hours, depending on which of us conducted it.

The Interview Method

Both of us have extensive interviewing experience, and agree about the style we strive to follow in administering interviews. We try to fit into the cultural milieu in which we are working. In India this means being more affective than in the United States. We adopted a host-guest relationship with the majority of our respondents. Virtually every respondent offered us something to eat or drink, either when we arrived or during the course of the interview. Occasionally, we felt great dismay when a respondent who could ill afford it nonetheless sent for Coca-Cola for us and our interpreter (not, of course, for himself). At 45 paise for a 6-ounce bottle, this hospitality could cost 20 per cent of a day's earnings. Other impoverished respondents, who could not even afford to serve us tea, would present us instead with large glasses of water. We were never certain which was greater: our gratitude at the gesture or our distress at having to consume at least one mouthful of the offering.

Some respondents insisted not only on providing us with coffee, tea, or Coke, but on feeding us as well. One such respondent lived in a village. He explained to us that because of his isolated location, we would be unable to find a "hotel" (the generic name for eating places not classy enough to be restaurants) and therefore would have to go without lunch if we did not accept his invitation. Fortunately, we did; for it soon became clear that his wife, daughters, and sisters-in-law had been cooking since the previous day in anticipation of our visit, but also that if we had declined, we would have passed up a sumptuous feast.

Similarly, we always offered tea or coffee and snacks to those respondents who preferred to come to our hotel to be interviewed. We tried not to conduct the interviews at the hotel, because we thought a view, and preferably a tour, of the respondent's operation was important. Occasionally, for the respondent's convenience, we did schedule the interview at our hotel; several other times, respondents appeared unexpectedly at our doorstep, thinking that was what we had meant them to do.

One or the other of us conducted every interview, assisted by an interpreter. The interpreter was unnecessary for some of the interviews, particularly in Tamilnadu, where many of the respondents spoke excellent English. For most of the Orissa interviews and in some areas of Tamilnadu and Punjab, however, an interpreter was essential. Both of us know enough of several north Indian languages so that our interpreters could not simply translate a fifteen minute answer as "He says 'no'." In Tamilnadu we were just lucky in having interpreters with a subtle knowledge of English and Tamil and a sensitive feel for doing research.

We did not hire a team of assistants to conduct interviews for us, although if had we might have collected more interviews. Apart from problems of training and supervising interviewers and avoiding "coffee house interviews," we insist on conducting interviews ourselves because we think one learns more that way. Let us illustrate with two examples.

One of us had just completed a lengthy interview, conducted in English, with a very interesting and pleasant respondent. This person was not only a successful manufacturer, but a very modern kind of man. His clean, new factory was well lit and well organized. His work operation was well organized, too, with an effective degree of task differentiation among the workers, the supervisors, and himself. In response to the "values" items in our questionnaire, he had given a completely nontraditional set of responses: he did not believe in astrology, he believed daughters should be educated to the same level as sons, and so forth—one of a very few respondents to answer all the items this way.

His factory was located in a newly developed area away from the main road, so when the interview was finished, he sent an errand boy to fetch a taxi. While we waited, we sat in the respondent's office, chatting with him. Looking around the room, we noticed a most unusual chest of drawers made of exquisitely-grained wood. Although the piece was of standard height, it had a curious feature: there were some fifteen drawers, ranging in depth from just a few inches to a foot or more. Since any kind of bureau is rare in India, we commented on how beautiful and unusual the piece was. The respondent explained that he had it made to order (not unusual for wooden furniture in India) according to his own careful set of specifications. "And did you notice the drawers?" he asked. We replied that we had wondered about their size. Proudly, he replied,

"That is so they can exactly accommodate all the different sizes of the bottles I store in them." It then turned out that he was a practitioner of ayurvedic medicine—the indigenous, traditional system, considered unscientific by practitioners of Western (allopathic) medicine—during the hours when his factory was closed. He usually treated people without change, as a service to the needly. The drawers of the bureau held his vast array of ayurvedic medicines.

The other of us, conducting an interview in an industrialized section, was surprised on entering the factory grounds to see an elephant there. The respondent turned out to be friendly and open, and also a "modern man." Since he seemed not to be in a hurry to end our meeting, we decided to ask about the elephant. "Oh, the elephant," said the respondent. "He belongs to our family. We have always kept elephants, although now we can afford only to keep one. We lend him out on ritual occasions to authorized religious groups who require an elephant and request us for him." Clearly, keeping an elephant is, for this respondent, an important way to fulfill a religious obligation.

These examples illustrate to us the importance, particularly in other societies, of doing interviews ourselves. In the context of questions about economic development and internalization of "modern" or "traditional" values, the ayurvedic medicines and the elephant become interesting data. We do not think these two, clearly "modern," men less modern for knowing these things about them. Rather, we think that the notion of "modernity" has been conceptualized rather unidimensionally, and there is more to this issue than meets most scholars' eyes.

In general, then, while recognizing that the debate between those who favor large-scale surveys and those who think the case study method more valid will probably never be satisfactorily resolved, we nonetheless come down heavily for the case method when dealing with qualitative data such as ours. Even taking into account the limitations of our samples (and not all large-scale surveys necessarily use excellent sampling techniques; see, e.g., Cantril, 1965), we are convinced that being confident one knows something, even though one many not be sure precisely how generally true it is, is preferable to being absolutely confident that one's findings are applicable to the entire population from which one has sampled, when the findings themselves are meaningless (for examples of the latter, see Eldersveld, Jaganadham, and Barnabas, 1968; Verba, Bhatt, and Ahmed, 1971).

Most respondents seemed equally willing to be interviewed by either of us. Some were even charmed by the idea of an Ameri can "lady sociologist." One respondent, however, specifically requested that his interview be conducted by Mr. Taub. Ordinarily, we made every effort to accede to respondents' requests, but in this case, Mr. Taub already had scheduled an interview for approxi mately the same hour in another part of town. Mrs. Taub and her female interpreter therefore arrived at the site of the interview to find a strict Muslim household, women of the family in purdah in another part of the building.

Worse still, the respondent—apparently disbelieving our claims of scholarly interest only—seemed to have decided that Mr. Taub was the advance guard of an American company looking for an Indian collaborator (several other of our respondents, unable to imagine why anyone might want to study small-scale industries, also came to this conclusion). When Mrs. Taub appeared, he was sure he had lost his opportunity. Nonetheless, he gamely went through with the interview, interspersing his answers to our ques tions with questions of his own about the condition of the Ameri can market for his product. He even went through with serving the lavish meal he had prepared for Mr. Taub to Mrs. Taub and her interpreter, though his discomfiture at having to eat his meal in the company of two women—one American and one Hindu—was obvious.

Interviewing in the Field

Before meeting the sampled respondents, we sent each a letter to inform him of our existence, what we were about, that we hoped to interview him, and the dates that we would be in his area. We timed the mailing of the letter so that it would reach the respon dent's workplace immediately before our arrival in his locality. We sent the letters to respondents in Orissa in two batches. The first batch was written in English. The second, prepared after finding a superb research assistant, were translated and written out by him in Oriya. In any case, it did not matter. Many of the letters were returned to us, either because the firm no longer existed, or because the addressee was unlocatable, or the address inadequate, or because the village was temporarily inaccessible. Many of the people we later interviewed did not remember receiving a letter, and the few who did thought it was odd, or wondered what it meant.

We had been irritated by the large number of returned letters until we set out ourselves to find the respondents. Then we learned that trying to locate the members of a sample in Orissa is a methodologist's nightmare. Trying to locate someone named Jaga-bandhu Moharana, whose address is given as Sagadia Sahi, Cuttack, is like trying to locate an American named John Smith when the only address one has for him is Haight-Ashbury, San Franscisco—and that address may be wrong.

We spent many a day in Cuttack city, driving, and walking, and taking cycle-rickshaws, down main roads and winding back alleys, trying to find our chosen respondents. In some cases, the respondent was no longer at the address we had, but neighbours could tell us that his business had failed and he had moved away, or that he had gotten a new workshop in another location. In other cases, the firm never had been at the address given by the directory, but someone in the area had heard if it and could tell us where to find it. In a few cases, no-one had ever heard of the person.

More puzzling were the cases in which we located a person of the right name in the right neighborhood, but because of details that came out in the interview, were then unsure whether this was the person listed in the directory. Perhaps he manufactured a different product and had never manufactured the one listed. Was the directory in error, or was this a different person? Or perhaps all the information corresponded except size of investment, or date of fouding of the enterprise. Since there are only a few different surnames in the area (and a limited number of first names are very popular, too), and since the neighborhoods are large, another person of the same name might easily live in the same area. On the other hand, the directory was in error often enough (our manufacturer of costumes and scenery, for example—who clearly was the correct respondent—was listed in the directory under "Principal Items of Manufacture" as "Printing") that we could not rely on its accuracy to resolve internal contradictions. There was simply no way, in some cases, to tell if we had found the right respondent. Asking the respondent was often no help, since many obviously correct respondents did not even know they were considered "registered," with their names listed in a book. Thus, they had no idea if they and the listed firm were one and the same (indeed, many could not figure out how we had found them, or why we had come to them).

Most of our Orissa sample was located in Cuttack city, but some were in Kendrapara, and some were in assorted villages in between. Therefore, we made a three day excursion up the Orissa coast to try to locate as many as possible of our village and Kendrapara sample members. In the end, of our sample of 56, we were able to interview 45, for a response rate in Orissa of 80 per cent.

After our experiences in Orissa, we were pleasantly startled to find a stack of mail awaiting us at our hotel in Madras city. Members of the sample, on receiving our letter, had immediately written to us, in some cases setting up appointments to meet us, and in others simply expressing their interest in the work and their willingness to be interviewed. The prompt replies to our letter were only the first example of the rather orderly style of life found in Madras. Firms had addresses that not only included street names, but also numbers. Many had telephones, so we could make appointments with them for interviews on a specified date and time. We were able to buy a map of the city. We had virtually none of the confused-identity problems that had plagued us in Orissa.

We found the greatest range of variation in respondents' social class in Madras, a range that correlated roughly with variations in size and sophistication of industry, and type of workplace. The industrial estate at Guindy (in Madras) hummed with activity. It was the site of large modern small-scale enterprises run by middle- or upper-middle class men who dressed in Western clothes and spoke excellent English. But Madras also had its share of sheet-metal workers, manufacturers of gates and grilles, vesselmakers, and the like. These were located far from the modern industrial estate, down muddy lanes and side streets. What we did not find as small-scale industries in Madras, however, were the tailors, traditional craftsmen, millers, and dry cleaners that had constituted such a large part of the registered small-scale sector in Orissa.

Here again, we were aware of the importance of conducting interviews ourselves. By doing so, we were able to interview 74 members of our sample out of the 80 chosen, for a response rate of 92.5 per cent. Equally importantly, we improved our credibility. One day, we visited an official of the Small Industries Development Corporation in his office. We had been to see this man before, and had found him pleasant enough, but rather brisk and uninformative. This time, we came to his office after a morning of interviewing. "So," he declared, "you have been seeing the factories in the industrial estate." A statement, not a question. "Yes," we said, "and also on Hood Wharf and in Choolai." We were referring to our sheet-metal workers and gate and grille fabricators. Clearly, the dirty and dilapidated areas to which we referred were places that scholars were not expected to go, for the official expostulated, "My God! Have you been even *there?*" At that point, the quality of the interview changed. Our conversation lasted more than an hour, and we learned a great deal about the management of small-scale industries in Tamilnadu.

Punjab lay midway between Orissa and Tamilnadu in ease of locating respondents, as well as in respondents' social class and in size and sophistication of industry. Streets in the new area of Ludhiana were named, as were the main roads, but not streets in the old. There, addresses were given as neighborhoods, much as they had been in Cuttack. Once again, many of our letters were returned, marked "Inadequate Address." Telephones were few, and so, correspondingly, were interview appointments made in advance. Since many of the firms were larger than those in Orissa, however, or at least had larger markets, people in the area nearby often recognized the company name and were able to direct us to it.

The populations included within the boundaries of Ludhiana city and Jullundur city had undergone almost incredible growth in the preceding twenty years. Ludhiana nearly tripled in size, from a population of 153,795 in 1951 to a population of 397,850 in 1971, with Jullundur nearly doubling, going from 168,816 to 296,106 in the same period (GOI, 1971b). As a result, the state lagged behind in providing the kinds of amenities found in industrial areas elsewhere. Paved streets were few, for example, and landscaping was nonexistent. When it rained, the industrial area became seas of mud. Sections of the city were submerged for a day or two. Cycle rickshaws could not go, so if one wanted to get somewhere, one took off his shoes and rolled up his pants legs—only a symbolic gesture, since the water was hip-deep—and slogged on. In the summer, these oceans turned to clouds of dust that whipped the hapless pedestrian.

The overarching fact of life in Punjab when we arrived in late November 1971 was the coming crisis between India and Pakistan over the future of East Bengal, the eastern part of Pakistan, which was later to become Bangladesh. Located on India's northwest boundary—the international crossover point is in Amritsar—Punjabis know they will be the first to be hit in case of an outbreak of hostilities between the two countries.

By this time, the outlines of American policy, "tilting" toward Pakistan, had become eminently clear. Officials in New Delhi had become increasingly hostile toward the American government (and, by extension, toward American citizens), but the hostility had not yet reached Punjab. More detrimental to the progress of interviewing than the respondents' attitudes toward us was their palpable tension at the prospect of war. Some people were frightened and anxious; others welcomed it as an opportunity to repay the Pakistanis for past brutalities.

The tension was well founded. We had been in Punjab only a week, and had completed about 15 interviews, when bombing began and the news announced war. By the time the war had ended, our time in India had run out, and we were obliged to return home to meet other commitments. To complete the interviewing, one of us returned to Punjab in the summer of 1972. By then, ironically, Punjabi attitudes toward Americans had caught up with the angry official reactions of our earlier visit (official attitudes had actually begun already to moderate); the hostility toward us was as thick as the sense of impending war had been six months before.

The difficulty of interviewing in such a setting was compounded by a heat wave of extraordinary duration and intensity. Temperatures remained at 120 degrees for days on end, and never dropped below 105 during the two months of our stay. The combination of the heat and the power failures made everyone ill-tempered. The physical discomfort was bad enough, but the need to suspend production for many hours each day was especially galling to these businessmen, and they were in no mood to talk to an American social scientist. "Why should I talk to you?" one asked. "You are our enemy." Taking a leaf from the Gandhian notebook, we just continued to sit there, perspiring silently. Only the obvious fact that we were suffering as much as they were led respondents to be willing to be interviewed. In the end, however, we were able to interview 74 of our 75 sample members, for a response rate in Punjab of 98.6 per cent.

In 1975, external forces again intervened. Mrs. Gandhi's declaration of emergency and her subsequent suspension of civil rights, crackdown on black money, and sudden arrests for political as well as economic reasons, made our respondents reluctant to talk about government policy. Several forces offset that difficulty, however. Anti-American sentiment had dissipated. Those who had feared we were agents of the Indian government felt more secure. Even though they had, on our first visit, discussed black market activity and perhaps other illegal acts as well, they had suffered no negative consequences. In fact, some warm personal relationships had grown up in the intervening period. We had sent all of the respondents an article we had written about small-scale industries (Taub and Taub, 1974) and many, in fact, had read it. All agreed with its general drift, and some made helpful criticisms. Almost all had shown it to their friends, government officials, and others. There is something pleasant about having foreign visitors drop in from time to time, and many greeted us as old friends. Most importantly, they had become trained respondents. We did not have to explain why we were there or convince respondents of our legitimacy.

Conclusion

We have gone into some detail about the social, political, and psychological milieux in which we conducted our research because we think such contexts are an integral part of the research process. Too often, reports of social research omit human elements, implying that the work was carried out in a clinical laboratory. For better or worse, however, the context of the research—the international situation, the weather, the state of the economy, conditions in the neighborhood, attitudes toward the interviewer—may have a direct bearing on the kinds and quality of data one collects. Further, the reactions and responses of interviewers to those conditions are themselves data.

This point does not simply apply to data collected in exotic foreign lands. A national research organization recently assisted one of us in doing research in a Chicago community. They reported, and we observed, the potential respondents' palpable terror as they hid behind locked doors. The interviewers became increasingly anxious about going into the neighborhood. All of this information was as important as the more formal data we collected from the interviews. Like it or not, the research environment can materially affect the research outcome and even, indeed, determine if there will be an outcome at all (cf., e.g., Wax, 1973).

CHAPTER FIVE

ENTREPRENEURIAL PROFILES: ORISSA

Located on India's east coast, approximately halfway down the subcontinent, Orissa is best known in India for its religious architecture and its miles of beautiful beaches. The city of Puri houses the temple of Lord Jaganath, an important pilgrimage center. Once a year, several hundred thousand visitors crowd this city of 60,000 to watch Lord Jaganath leave the temple, hauled in a large cart (hence the English word "juggernaut") by devotees to another, smaller temple. Puri and Gopalpur, further down the coast, are also the sites of elegant, old-fashioned resort hotels.

Almost half of Orissa's population lives in the state's four coastal (of thirteen) districts; in 1975, the total population was 22 million. Along the coast is the rich alluvial soil associated everywhere with deltaic areas, and the frequent devastating flooding that accompanies it. The state's highest population concentrations, between 400 and 800 people per square mile, are in these coastal districts, which are also the state's major agricultural areas. Much of the rice produced here is shipped to West Bengal to the north. The state is also an important source of fish for West Bengal. The interior of Orissa is the former site of numerous small, independent kingdoms known as "princely states." This region is physically inhospitable, but is inhabited by a large tribal population.

At that time of the study, two very large factories had recently been built in Orissa. In the northwestern corner of the state lies Rourkela, one of India's three major steel plants, constructed with German collaboration. In the southwest is a MiG aircraft assembly plant constructed with Russian assistance. At Paradip, in the northeast, the state had recently constructed a port used in shipping its iron ore, which is mined extensively.

Cuttack is the state's largest city, with a 1975 population of 305,000. Just as the entire state has a rural quality, however, so

Cuttack city itself feels to the visitor more like a congeries of small towns than it does like a small city. The main streets are broad, unpaved, and lined with shops; behind them lie thousands of tortuous paths, snaking their way into hundreds of village-like enclaves. The principal means of transportation are bicycles, bicycle-rickshaws, and feet. There are no tall buildings, no department stores, nothing one associates with urban life except crowds. Political life in Orissa has been complex. From 1947 to 1958, one could most easily understand the situation by dividing the political world into two groups: the Congress Party, dominated by the coastal people, and the Ganatantra Parishad (now Swatantra), dominated by the princes of Orissa's formerly independent states. Since 1958, however, state politics have been characterized by shifting coalitions among political leaders of various stripes, highlighted by periodic collapses of the government, followed by rule from New Delhi when no local leader can form a government.

Orissa ranks low among the states not only in number of small industries, but on most measures of prosperity. In 1975, 94 per cent of its population was classified as rural, more than in any other state. With 20 per cent of its population literate, it ranked eleventh among seventeen. It was twelfth in income per capita (GOI, 1970: 38). Orissa is not only poor, it is conservative. Although the Orissan temples are important tourist attractions, they remain virtually the only major Indian temples that resist allowing foreigners—even those certified by Indian authorities to be orthodox Hindus—inside even their outer walls. That this sentiment has persisted despite national legislation to the contrary and, on occasion, very great pressure from political leaders is an indicator of the strength of traditional feelings and the power of those who hold them.

Taken as a whole, then, Orissa is a poor state, ranking toward the bottom of India's states on many dimensions. Its general situation is replicated in the small-scale industrial sector.

The Small-Scale Industries

"If you can learn why Orissa is so inhospitable to industry, you will have performed a great service," a young lawyer told us. "Industries here always wither and then die, even those that have had brief periods of prosperity."

A mood of depression compounded by lassitude hung over much of Orissa's industry. One begins there to understand better the self-reinforcing character of a depressed economy and the fragility of enterprise in such a setting. Orissa had neither the capital resources to sustain privately-owned industry nor the purchasing power to provide adequate nongovernment consumption. Most successful companies were run by businessmen who earned their money elsewhere and were looking for a new investment, or by those who already had access to large markets such as Calcutta or Madras. So delicate was the economic balance on which many businesses were built that small changes, for example, in government policy, could generate radical changes in fortune.

The depressed state of Orissa's industries was quickly apparent to an observer. Its major industrial estate was half vacant, the empty sheds monuments to numerous failed enterprises. At the time of our first visit, a once-prosperous medium-scale industry manufacturing automobile batteries had just collapsed, a result of being dropped from the State Trading Corporation's list of authorized suppliers. Without the export business channeled to it by STC, the company could not stay alive. Many of the other companies on the industrial estate operated only marginally. In 1971, a supposed manufacturer of bicycles gained most of his income from renting cycle-rickshaws, assembled at his plant, to laborers on a daily basis. Still other manufacturers derived their income primarily from selling their controlled-price raw material allocations on the black market.

On our return to Orissa in 1975, the picture had not brightened substantially. Of the firms most prosperous in 1971, a few remained so; but others were on the economic margin, and one was just about to go out of business.

To choose 56 companies for our Orissa sample in 1971, we had to draw 82 names from the *Directory of Industries* compiled in 1967. Of the 82, 13 had definitely failed, another 7 were unknown to people in the neighborhood, 2 had to be replaced because they were cooperatively owned, and 2 had to be replaced because they were large-scale industries. Of the 45 industrialists we were finally able to locate and interview, 3 had gone out of business, 5 more were failing, and another 20 were barely holding their own.

In all, 10 respondents of the 45 could be called prosperous. Eight of these had accrued their capital in areas other than the industry for which we interviewed them. Seven had followed the classic Third-World pattern (and the pattern of developing Germany in the nineteenth century), earning their wealth in commerce and turning to industry as another source of opportunity. Of the 10, 5 came to Orissa from outside of the state, and still relied on their outside contacts for marketing. Three others belonged to minority groups—2 were Muslims and one's mother tongue was Telugu, the language of the adjacent state to the south—leaving only 2 who were unambiguously part of mainstream Orissan culture. If Orissa were the only state we had studied, we would have been tempted to attribute some defect to "native" populations in India, emphasizing the virtues of pariah (in the Western sense) capitalism and suggesting either that migrants had more vitality because they uprooted themselves to seek better opportunities, or that the uprooting process itself might free one from the weight of traditional ties, making innovation easier. All of this may in some measure be true, but the patterns were certainly different in the other two states.

The most well-to-do person in our sample, and certainly one of the wealthiest in the entire state, was a Marwari—a member of a business community whose origins are the inhospitable desert lands of Rajasthan. Marwaris have migrated all over India, succeeding in trade, in moneylending, and to an extent, in manufacturing. This man's factories, located in a village (on a railway line) near rich deposits of fire clay, produced glasses, bottles, fire bricks, and ceramic bathroom fixtures. The glass products were sold primarily in south India; the others had an all-India market. The manufacturer also held the Orissa franchise for Coca-Cola. He made the Coke bottles in his glass factory. In addition, he owned rental property. This respondent acknowledged a gross annual income for all of his factories combined of more than Rs. 20 million, and an overall investment in machinery and raw materials of approximately the same amount. His three large factories, which employed about 4,000 workers, extended over fifty acres, dominating the village.

He appeared in our sample because he owned, in partnership with the Government of Orissa, a fourth factory established to manufacture ceramic tiles. This factory, a small-scale unit with an investment of Rs. 750,000 in machinery and raw materials, was created as a demonstration project to encourage others to set up similar enterprises and to provide local employment. It was a failure. Its imported machinery was allegedly defective, producing ripples and bubbles in many of the tiles. The defective tiles could have been sold in an expanding construction market, our respondent reported, but were bypassed in the market at that time because better tiles were readily available. The machinery lay idle; the factory building was used to store the Coke bottles.

After Marwaris, the largest group of traders and merchants in our sample came from the state of Gujarat. They were an austere group—strict vegetarians, teetotalers, and not given to display. Their religious beliefs have much in common with those of the Gujarati Jains, whom Weber (1958b: 199–201ff.) Singles out as a group whose ideology had consequences for capital accumulation much like those of Calvinist Protestantism. This group, too, has migrated all over India. One of the two Gujaratis in our sample was among the 10 most prosperous. His small factory, however, was but a sideline, supplying simple bicycle parts to his family shop. He also owned a large and successful general store, as well as property.

Two men from Bengal were in this prosperous group. One, a soap manufacturer, sold his product primarily in the large Calcutta market. The other operated a successful sawmill. The mill about which we interviewed him was one of several owned by his family, who were also successful timber contractors, licensed to harvest timber from the forests. The soap manufacturer was a grocery and soap wholesaler in Calcutta before he entered manufacturing. The sawmill operator began his mill after establishing a career in the timber trade.

The fifth successful respondent was another non-Oriya, one of three Punjabis in our Orissa sample. He and his brothers, refugees displaced after Partition, came to Orissa with little but energy and mechanical skill. The respondent came first, at the invitation of a raja who had hired him to set up a sugar mill but was deposed soon after. He realized he would have to do something on his own, so he sent for his brothers to join him. Each of the brothers had received a small sum from the government's refugee relief fund after Partition. Pooling their resources, they built an ice factory in a village 90 miles north of Cuttack city, near a major source of fish. Fishermen used the ice to chill their catch while shipping it to distant markets, and the brothers flourished. Then, climatic conditions changed and the fish changed their habitat. The brothers lost their market for ice, so they converted the ice factory into a cold storage unit. Since local farmers did not at that time plant any crop that required cold storage, the brothers canvassed the countryside distributing seed and persuading farmers to plant potatoes that might then be held in the cold storage after harvest. When a nearby oceanfront area was developed into a port, the brothers opened a restaurant there. They had run a gas station near the ice factory, but it was bypassed by a national highway built to carry iron ore to the new port. This family reported its gross annual income from all its enterprises as Rs. 250,000.

Two of the minority-group successes were Muslims, of which there were 7 among our Orissa respondents. Although Muslims can be found in most occupations in India, they dominate leather, rubber, and tobacco products. That Muslims are active in the leather trade is not surprising. Leatherwork is an unclean occupation for Hindus; untouchables constitute the only other large group of 'leatherworkers. The manufacture of rubber products seems to have evolved from the skills and techniques required in leatherwork. Then too, similar products—sandals, for example, as well as industrial supplies such as flexible couplings—can be made from either of these materials.

The affinity of Muslims for the manufacture of tobacco products is not so easily explained, but is undeniable. Three such firms appear in our three-state sample, two of them in Orissa—a manufacturer of a tobacco-based product that is mixed with molasses, lime powder, and numerous secret ingredients for use as toothpaste, called *gurakhu;* a producer of inexpensive leaf-wrapped cigarettes (*bidi*); and a manufacturer of a product chewed after meals for its refreshing taste, made of chopped betel nuts mixed with spices or tobacco, called *seeval* or *supari.* The owners of all three enterprises were Muslims. The *gurakhu* manufacturer, whose family has manufactured this product for over a hundred years, reported annual sales, almost all of them in Calcutta, of Rs. 3.5 million. The second prosperous Muslim repaired and retreaded tires. He also had income from extensive property holdings.

The last of the well-to-do minority-group manufacturers was a family that made gold jewelry and sold it in their retail shop. Their mother tongue was Telugu. The family came from an area within what is politically Orissa but culturally belongs to Andhra Pradesh. This enterprise did not entail manufacturing. Rather than producing the jewelry, the family subcontracted their orders to village goldsmiths who handcrafted the jewelry. The family devoted most of their own energies to running the store, the largest of its kind in Cuttack.

The remaining 2 of the 10 prosperous manufacturers were both native to Orissa and spoke Oriya as their mother tongue. The first was a baker who manufactured biscuits (cookies) and "double-roti" (white bread) for the local market. Every day, his fleet of rickshaws and his truck rushed freshly baked goods to local shops. The baker was the only manufacturer in our Orissa sample who succeeded by providing consumer goods solely for local consumption. He reported an annual gross income of Rs. 1.4 million on an investment of Rs. 500,000. He entered the bakery business after participating in a family-owned wholesale grocery business, and he continued to have an interest in that enterprise.

The second had the exclusive Orissa agency for several popular products of which the government was a major purchaser. He reported his gross annual income as Rs. 10.8 million in 1971. Although he had remained in business for a long time, his most successful periods were when men he supported held important political office. Then, government agencies were ordered to purchase his products, even if these were not entirely appropriate to their needs. When his mentors lost office, his fortunes declined. For some time, he had run two other small-scale industries, one of which sold almost its entire output to the government, and the other of which sold a substantial amount to the government. In addition, the respondent had obtained government certification as an approved supplier for the second industry. Approved suppliers must be used by non-government enterprises purchasing products with government loans. Since the list of such suppliers may be very short (depending on the particular product) and potential buyers numerous, such certification was highly coveted.

Both Oriya respondents knew that they were exceptional, and the second was bitter about it. "You cannot do business in Orissa," he said. "The government is run by foreigners (people from outside the state) and they do not have the best interests of the people at heart. The only people who thrive here are outsiders—Punjabis, Marwaris, and Bengalis. The rest of us suffer, and government officials do not care." At the time of our first interview, in fact, he had just wound up his two small firms. The government had begun to manufacture the first product itself, and the respondent's second firm had been removed from the list of approved suppliers when a new political group came to power. This respondent's fortunes were on the decline; when we returned in 1975, he was selling his last firm and going out of business for good.

Industries and Politics

Although political chicanery plays an important part in the prosperity of many private individuals in India and, probably, in most democratic capitalist nations as well, its impact in Orissa was particularly visible and dramatic, because other sources of successful industrial growth were so meager. Other of our respondents had tied their fortunes to political leaders in Orissa with even less success than that of the respondent just described. In general, they enjoyed brief periods of prosperity, but because they established their firms when their friends came to power, they never learned either how to manufacture their product efficiently or how to compete for business in the marketplace. Consequently, when their mentors left office, their industries floundered.

The government was the largest purchaser of goods and services in Orissa, and its spending rippled widely through the economy. Everyone waited for government orders, with little opportunity to make real money otherwise, so the impact of the government's decisions were more marked. When the state was constructing Paradip Port and the connecting superhighway, anyone who owned a moving vehicle thrived. Even people who did not own a vehicle bid on the contracts to transport ore. On the strength of being awarded such a contract, they were able to purchase one or more trucks on credit, repaying the loan from the money they made on the job.

All of the prosperous respondents except the Muslims had political connections that were essential to the conduct of their businesses. Some of them engaged in outright fraud. Others made generous political contributions to get scarce raw materials. Everyone needed the cooperation of the government in one way or another. The soap manufacturer needed mutton tallow and other oils, and the baker needed flour, sugar and cellophane. The government provided the allocations of or licenses to obtain these and all other scarce raw materials. The glass manufacturer set up his tile factory in partnership with the government. He needed them to grant licenses for the machinery he imported. The Punjabi did not need help from the government, but he contributed regularly to all political candidates to insure that the government would not interfere in his operation regardless of who won. There was simply no way to manufacture in Orissa without being involved, formally or informally, with the government.

The Other Industries

Most of the remaining enterprises in our Orissa sample were hardly industries at all. Many were run by craftsmen working to order. They had no capital to produce inventories or even to buy raw materials for the items they contracted to produce. Many were listed in the industries directory by government officials trying to enhance their own appearance as zealous performers.

Some of these industries might more properly be called services. A customer would bring an item to the businessman, who would do something to it and return it. In this category were 3 tailors, 1 dry cleaner, 1 electric motor repairman, 1 musical instrument repairman, 3 printers, and 8 millowners. Let us look more closely at this last category.

Seven of the mills were located in villages. For about Rs. 3,000 one could in 1975 buy the basic milling machine and connect it to a power line. Local agriculturalists would bring their grain, mostly rice, to the miller and wait while it was hulled, watching closely to be certain that none was stolen. Such businesses are seasonal and depend on agricultural yields. Two were languishing. One's electricity had been disconnected because he had not earned enough money to pay the bill, and did not know he was eligible for a concessional rate as a seasonal user. He had borrowed money from a moneylender to buy the machine, and was sinking more deeply into debt. He was trying to earn the money to repay the loan by doing day labor.

A second miller was a victim of progress. He failed because a former official of the Department of Industries had taken a loan from his sometime employer and opened a mill down the road. The new mill used more modern machinery, and could process a variety of agricultural products such as coconut and split peas in addition to rice. This modern mill was thriving, with machinery whirring and a long line at the door. We began our interview there, thinking it was the mill in our sample. Only later did we learn that the nearby dilapidated building whose owner languished on a bench in front was the mill we sought.

Seven of the eight millers in our sample provided traditional services in a traditional context, although more efficiently than the old hand-pounders did. They did not have enough capital to buy grain, process it, and sell it in the market themselves, and none of the seven had more than one employee. The rural setting was brought home in the course of interviewing one of the millers. It was a long walk to the interview, and since a foreign social scientist, interpreter in tow, is a novelty, we were soon followed by most of the residents (an experience we became accustomed to after a while). We therefore had to conduct the interview in front of a large crowd. A snake charmer came by, playing his flute as the sun set, shadows lengthened, and his cobra undulated. A group of women returned from the forest, where they had been collecting wood all day, heads piled high with twigs that they would sell in the village. They leaned their bundles up against walls and trees, sat down to rest, and watched the snake, the crowd, and us. One should not, however, equate the bucolic nature of the setting with a conception of timeless, changeless India. The lone dirt road to this village led straight to the gates, a mile away, of the large glass factory we described earlier.

The eighth miller had located his facility in Cuttack city. His milling operation was tied to his wholesale business. He was the only one who had enough capital to purchase grain, process it, and then sell it on the market. He was doing quite well financially, although less so than the 10 most prosperous respondents. His approach to his enterprise was modern: he estimated costs, had located his mill according to a thought-out plan, and chose his processes within the framework of the market. A Marwari, he was the only miller not working in his native village. His overview of the grain business and his detailed grasp of the national situation contrasted markedly with the orientation of the village millers.

A step up in the industrial scale were our 6 furniture manufacturers, whose factories were huddled together in one section of Cuttack city. Five of them were carpenters who bid for small government contracts to make furniture for offices and for the fancy guest houses the government maintains for traveling officials. Winning such a contract usually required a bribe of 10 to 15 per cent of the total award. They then had to borrow money at 25 per cent interest per month to buy raw materials. They were better off with an occasional contract to provide furniture for a newly married couple. In those cases, they demanded an advance payment, which they would use to buy their materials. All were following in the footsteps of their fathers, and they found it difficult to imagine what else they might do or might have done. Working and living together, some of them relatives, they all knew about government contracts to be let and bargains in raw materials.

Only one of the carpenters could be considered an innovator, and then only because he was pushed into the carpentry business by misfortune. He was the son of a former landlord (zamindar) who lost some of his property through land reform and some to political agitation prior to Independence. After the respondent failed his examination for the B.A., he made a stab at the trucking business, but was fleeced by employees who claimed that sound parts were defective. The employees sold the original parts, replacing them with inferior ones for which they received kickbacks. The business failed, and the respondent, in desperation, decided to set up a furniture factory, because it seemed to him to be a business with a large profit margin per unit of sale, and one that was simple enough so employees would be unable to cheat him. At the peak of the 1971 season, when government contracts were let at the end of the fiscal year, he had 17 employees, most of whom brought their own tools. Although his shop was located with those of the other carpenters, neither he nor any of his employees was of their caste, and he stood apart from their close-knit group.

Because so much of his work was delegated, he was able—unlike the other carpenters—to spend most of his time soliciting business. His business was the only one that was at all differentiated in function. He began the business with an investment of Rs. 500 and by 1971 had bought land and constructed a building for Rs. 35,000.

In 1971, we had singled this manufacturer out because his firm seemed to have the rudiments of a modern enterprise: he was educated, the enterprise had differentiated functions, and growth seemed modest but steady. We anticipated that if any of the less-successful industries were going to take off, this would be the one. Returning in 1975, we initially congratulated ourselves on the accuracy of our prediction. The firm was humming, filling a government order for several hundred cabinets for television sets. In the interim, the owner had bought large chunks of the surrounding land, as well as a compressor, a spray painter, a welding machine, a guider, and two circular saws where there had not been a single power tool before. Lumber lay everywhere, as did cabinets at varying stages of completion. Annual gross revenue had increased from Rs. 70,000 to Rs. 300,000, and the number of employees had grown comparably.

Observing this prosperous scene, we made a note to emphasize the importance of differentiation in industrial organizations if they are to grow. Later in the week, quite by coincidence, we learned that the owner had taken a silent partner: the brother of a minister in the Orissa government. So much, we said, for organization theory. Here again was a case of an individual succeeding because of his ties to political allies who could funnel resources and contracts to him. We had outlined this process in 1971: a firm began modestly; then business and profits suddenly soared, and dropped off just as suddenly. The owners never learned how to run a factory for sustained growth. Consequently, when their political allies were out of favor, they were unable to remain in business. Even though some of these men became wealthy through their businesses they made no long-term contribution to the industrial development of the state. This cabinet maker was, by 1975, in the soaring phase; if the experience of others is a guide, his firm was soon to plummet.

One cannot write off entirely the importance of the characteristics that gained the owner his present prosperity. His middle-class origins gave him access to officialdom. As a manager rather than a craftsman, he had time to cultivate government officials and to seek business in other quarters. He was not mired, as the other carpenters were, in the process of making the goods; consequently, he could plan, organize, and innovate. Indeed, this level of organization was necessary to succeed even with the boon of political influence, and it may be sufficient to sustain the industry after the owner's political partner is out of power.

Tradition and Modernity in Industry

In industries such as these, many sharp distinctions between modern industries and traditional crafts blur, and this blurring helps us to understand the complexity associated with the word "modern," even in the relatively unambiguous context of a factory. A dramatic example of this complexity was the owner of a *chitralaya*, an "abode of pictures," which is a shop that manufactuers costumes and scenery to rent for local theatrical events, traveling theaters, and dance troupes. This respondent first learned about *chitralayas* when he worked in one in his village. In this poor area, costumers and set designers took advances so they could buy the materials to fabricate the stylized sets and costumes required for these rural performances.

Our respondent later moved to Cuttack city, where he opened a *chitralaya* of his own, catering to a wider range of customers. By 1975, he was the most successful in the city, providing costumes and sets even to those few Orissa artists who have become international figures and carry their own equipment with them abroad. He had systematically set out to build up his stock of costumes and sets so that they could be rented on demand, without the delays of fabricating to order. He also developed systems for moving the equipment from one troupe to another quickly, so that he did not lose money while gear stood idle. At the time of the first interview, he had applied to the Department of Industries for a loan so that he could increase his stock of supplies and improve his methods of moving the materials from one group to another.

The traditional roots of this business are obvious. The theater for which the respondent provided equipment was devoted to recreating ancient Hindu religious tales in highly stylized form. Further, the owner of the company was one of only two Brahmins in our Orissa sample. (The other was a printer.) While operating a *chitralaya* cannot at all be considered this man's "traditional occupation," nonetheless, it is a more consistent choice than many others might be. Brahmins, in Hindu belief, are associated with and in principle responsible for both the conduct of religious ritual and for education. The connection to the *chitralaya* seems apparent. Likewise, printing was, in all our states, an occupation heavily populated by Brahmins. This too is not a traditional occupation, but it is an acceptable one, probably because of its association with literacy and the written word.

The idea of modernity in the industrial context is usually tied closely to the use of machinery and the conversion of inanimate fuels into power. Yet we have seen in our sample that almost all the millers, for example, who certainly use power-driven machinery, are only modern in any sense *because* they use that machinery. They were embedded in their villages, following family or caste occupations, providing traditional services in return for traditional forms of remuneration, and serving a narrowly defined, bounded clientele. By contrast, the owner of the *chitralaya,* who did not use power-driven machinery, nonetheless developed a differentiated organization, rationalized and responsive to market conditions. He attempted to use modern business management techniques (although he would not call them that) to increase both his custom and his profits. Similarly, the one prosperous carpenter who had just installed machinery had begun to develop the rudiments of a differentiated organization and, consequently, had taken a first step down a road that could conceivably transform furniture-making in Orissa.

In our sample also were men who used power-driven machinery to produce traditional farm tools and cooking utensils. In Tamilnadu, one such manufacturer collected his raw materials—old, worn-out utensils—through networks of small shops that took them in exchange for new pots. This manufacturer melted the old utensils down, cast them into ingots, and rolled them through his rolling machines. He then cut and stamped them on a sequence of power-driven presses. Since the pots were not his own raw materials, he was paid only for the operations he performed. After making them into new utensils, he redistributed them through the same network. Like the millers in Orissa, his relationship to his raw materials, and to his clients, was as traditional as if the work had been done by hand.

Conversely, one of our respondents, a graduate of Cambridge, manufactured electronic components. These components, however, were assembled by semiskilled workers entirely by hand. Even the soldering iron used to fuse the parts was heated in a fire, rather than by electricity. Much of Japan's industrial growth in the electronics field was driven by just such arrangements (Shinohara, 1968).

The point is that industrial technology is only one of a number of variables that may in combination be important for understanding what modernity of industrial organization means. The "modernity" or "traditionality" of the product may count, but in other contexts the organization of the work may make it modern; and modern organization may provide the entrepreneur with a distinct competitive advantage. Weber understood this well (1958a: 67ff.). Many of his intellectual successors, however have not.

Uncertainty

Fatalism is often thought to be an element of traditional Hinduism, and we found this orientation toward the future among many of our poorer respondents. Many commented on the uncertainty of the future, and we were struck by a "psychology of scarcity," with its fear of bad days ahead, that was most marked among our Orissa respondents. Even the most economically successful respondent in Orissa, the glass manufacturer, reported:

> Father always told me, one must build in such a way that he is always protected in his weakest position. That is, he can manage well in his worst possible time. Suppose I am doing ten lakhs (Rs. 1 million) worth of business. I should not live at the ten lakhs level. For some misfortune may befall us in our business, and then I will be wretched. So I must live at the one lakh level, which I know is the minimum possible income I can have. . . . My business may have different fortunes, but I will not lose everything.

This respondent is considering constructing several widely dispersed plants because he anticipates labor trouble in the future, and this is one way to halt its spread.

Uncertainty coupled with a sense of potential scarcity is firmly based in reality. Life abounds with potential disasters, made by both man and nature. We have already mentioned some ways in which the rhythms—sometimes vagaries—of government activity affect industrial life in Orissa. Other government activities, however, also have consequences. The tire retreader in our Orissa sample, for example, has not bothered to uncrate the new high-speed retreading machine he purchased from Czechoslovakia, because the government has decided to start its own tire retreading factory. Once the government's factory is operating, all government retreading jobs will be performed there. Similarly, government demonstration programs on how to start up leather-goods factories put many leatherworkers out of business.

Government factories may or may not be well run, but they always have the power to require that other government units purchase only from them. One unit in Orissa had to close because the government began to make and distribute the simple medicines that had been its product. Likewise, respondents feared the effects of nationalization, or at least of increasingly confiscatory taxation, on their futures. Many respondents decided not to let their firms grow too large to avoid becoming visible and, consequently, targets for takeover, increased government scrutiny, or inordinate demands for political contributions.

Recurrent social instability also made the respondents uneasy. Communal riots in the mid-1960s, for example, had serious economic consequences for the Muslims in Orissa. One tailor told us that he had expanded to the point where he was ready to install a showroom, a try-on room, and begin making ready-to-wear clothing. He lost most of his machines and other equipment during the riots, and became too discouraged to try for that level of achievement again.

Similarly, the *gurakhu* manufacturer had high walls, with heavy steel doors, around his factory. Guards stood at the entrance. He was consciously restricting production of his goods. He reported that the demand for his product would have enabled him, if he wished, to hire half again as many employees, even if he did not have the finances in hand—which he did. Instead, he had working for him only those people who did not try to sabotage his equipment during the last few bouts of communal rioting. He did not know of any other test that would guarantee him safety if the riots started again. Over the previous three years, he had had to develop an allocation system for customers, since demand so greatly exceeded production. (In some measure, the company had always restricted production. The product has a short shelf life, and by keeping it in limited supply, the firm was able to guarantee its freshness.) Like the glass manufacturer, this respondent toyed with the idea of opening factories in other states. Communal riots are usually localized, and with factories in other areas, he knew he would be able to continue manufacturing elsewhere even if the Orissa plant were shut down.

Nature, too, exacts a high toll from people in Orissa. We have mentioned flooding in the area, but this is not as serious a concern for businesses as are the regular hurricanes (or cyclones, as these oceanic storms are known in India) that visit the coastal region. In the Kendrapara area, several respondents mentioned that they were only, in 1971, beginning to recover from the devastating effects of the cyclone of 1968. The day after we left that part of the state, another cyclone struck, killing thousands of people and displacing many thousands more. Our assistant tried to visit the area shortly after the disaster, and learned that people we had intended to interview were dead. Whole villages had vanished; travel through the region was virtually impossible.

The cyclones had long-term effects as well. Ocean and river bottoms changed, causing the fish to leave. The livelihoods of many local fishermen, as well as of those (including one of our respondents) whose businesses depended upon the annual catch, were destroyed.

Under such circumstances, one is impressed not by the fatalism of the inhabitants, but by the willingness of so many to rebuild and try again. The ice manufacturer who converted his plant to a cold storage facility is one example. So is the Muslim manufacturer of cast concrete products, whose factory was destroyed by the 1968 cyclone. He was proud that in just three years, he had built his business back to the level it had attained prior to the cyclone. We do not know what effect the 1971 cyclone had on him.

In contrast to these adaptive, venturesome men, other respondents had only a limited sense of life's possibilities. In some ways, they parallel the small American shopkeepers described by Mayer and Goldstein (1961) and Vidich and Bensman (1959). One of the metalworkers in our sample hoped that if he made more and more goods, in greater variety, customers would start to come. (Vidich and Bensman's shopkeepers added more and more to their product lines.) He filled the street in front of his store with merchandise to attract the attention of customers; but his location was not very good—although it was the best he could afford—and few people passed by his shop.

The miller who watched all his customers go to the new, multipurpose mill down the lane is in much the same position as the small American grocer who loses his customers to the supermarkets (see Malamud, 1957). We emphasize the American comparison here, because the behavior of many of our respondents— despite their alleged traditionalism and the supposedly massive cultural differences between them and contemporary Americans— can, in fact, be understood, as their American counterparts can, by reference to objective circumstances, without resort to elaborate culturally-based explanations. The ranges of behavior in both countries are very great, a fact often missed by those who use idealized formulations of "modern" and "traditional" when making comparisons.

Conclusions

One must be wary of ascribing a constellation of attributes and behaviors to people just because they may appear traditional on one obvious dimension. Lerner (1964), Inkeles (1974), and others see traditional people as having a limited perception both of their own world and of the world outside; but as with the village we described earlier, that looked so timeless and changeless when we saw it, but whose residents worked in the glass factory, things may not always be only what they seem. One may be too eager to push people into categories that fit one's theoretical (and sometimes stereotypical) conceptions, the more so when the people themselves, eager to please, cater to those preconceptions. Let us illustrate.

In its efforts to augment the number of firms included in the directory, the Orissa Department of Industries had included a horn carver. He was an artisan who bought cattle horns, which he polished and carved into shapes both useful (pocket combs, pillboxes) and decorative (animal and other figurines). Sitting with his family in his little shop, carving and polishing, he looked every bit the ancient craftsman. His family worked seven days a week to produce goods that do not sell in great volume. In his interview, he communicated a sense of limited opportunity. Nonetheless, he had entered his best work in a national contest, and he won several prizes. He knew about the government handicraft stores scattered throughout India and in large cities over the rest of the world. His goods were displayed for sale in them. He had managed to borrow Rs. 1,000 from the state Handicrafts Board. He knew about export licenses. If he had had the resources, he would have printed a catalogue and price list for customers who could not come to his shop. His daughter was married to an engineer, and he planned for some of his sons to get government jobs.

This respondent began the interview by emphasizing that he was just a humble craftsman following his traditional occupation. Since both he and his shop fit that description in appearance, someone looking for "traditionalism" might easily be misled into romanticizing the life of craftsmen in India, or reading more into the appearance than in fact was there.

Summary

Orissa's small-industry activity corresponds closely to the state's overall economic position. As in many other parts of the third world, most of its successful businessmen are merchants and traders who have expanded their enterprises into industry. Other businessmen lack resources for investment, and potential customers lack disposable income to buy consumer goods. Industries that succeed in Orissa must therefore have access to capital and markets outside the state. Because of the poverty and the uncertain environment in which they operate, many of the businessmen in Orissa are constrained by a limited opportunity structure.

We are led, further, to recognize that conceptions of traditionalism and modernity must be multidimensional. Industries that use traditional means of production or manufacture traditional products may, nonetheless, have modern organizational structures. Others using modern machinery may make traditional goods or sell their products through traditional networks. Further, modern products may be produced by traditional means. We would not want to be obliged to locate any of these enterprises on a single traditional-modern continuum. |

CHAPTER SIX

ENTREPRENEURIAL PROFILES: TAMILNADU

Tamilnadu, like Orissa, is a coastal state with broad, sandy beaches, palm trees, and paddy fields; but there the similarity ends. This state, with its plentiful arable land, high rates of literacy, and numerous major industries, is one of India's more prosperous. The city of Madras, India's fourth largest with a population of 2.5 million in 1975, has broad avenues, bustling vehicular traffic, stately British-era administrative buildings, and new skyscrapers. Behind the boulevards are neighborhoods of narrow, winding streets congested with people, animals, and machines.

Madras is the home of some of India's largest industrial corporations, including, in the 1970s, one of the nation's three automobile manufacturers, one of the top three producers of bicycles, one of its few manufacturers of motorcycles, and manufacturers of tires, railway cars, and machine tools. Tamilnadu was the leading state in the manufacture of textiles and ranked fourth in industrial production, behind Maharashtra, West Bengal, and Gujarat. Its 44 million people were second in India in literacy and in degree of urbanization. This state was first in number of villages electrified but, surprisingly, ninth in per capita income.

Caste has consistently been an explicit and overt political issue in Tamilnadu, unlike many other states. Political power shifts between the Congress party and the local DMK (Dravida Munnetra Kazagham, or Southern Peasant's Party), which is anti-Brahmin and opposed to the establishment of Hindi as the national language. Brahmins in Tamilnadu, although only a small proportion of the population, have historically been a dominant group, overrepresented as large landowners, lawyers, doctors, professors, and civil servants. Non-Brahmins, hostile towards Brahmins because of their power, are also hostile to them because they believe Brahmins are not true South Indians, but descendents of invaders from the north. Consequently, the anti-Brahmin spirit in Madras has a populist flavor that seeks to redistribute Brahmin wealth, reduce Brahmin representation in the professions and civil services in favor of the dispossessed little man, and dilute the Brahmin cultural hegemony that is reinforced by high, Sanskritic Hinduism. These attitudes have affected the pattern of small-scale industrial development in the state.

Small manufacturing firms are located throughout Madras city. Many of the prosperous ones are to be found on the industrial estates, one of which—Guindy—was the first in India. Guindy's paved street, leafy trees, and seeded lawns give it a park-like aspect. The government's Small-Scale Industries Office has a library specializing in economics and industrial affairs there.

Many other firms, particularly the smaller and low-technology ones, cluster in specialized enclaves within the city. Metal shapers hammer out utensils, trunks, and buckets along Hood Wharf, Wall Tax Road, and Iron Monger Street. Hide tanners and merchants have their own corner of the city. Other enterprises congregate in the city's older commercial districts, and still others are spread around outlying areas. To shape the development of new types of industries, the government of Tamilnadu constructed a series of functionally specialized industrial estates, each of which was to provide for a single type of industry, such as electronics. At the time of the study, however, functionally related industries had not grouped themselves together in any meaningful way.

Comparing small industries in Tamilnadu with those in Orissa, one finds some similarities. Nine owners of small enterprises in our sample of 75 (12 per cent) came originally from the states of Gujarat, Punjab, and Rajasthan. Unlike Orissa, however, these "outsiders" did not dominate the Tamilnadu industrial scene; indeed, only one of this group is in the most prosperous stratum of our sample. As in Orissa, basic metal shaping enterprises were the most numerous (about 15 per cent). As in Orissa in 1971, we found nonexistent and nonproducing industries whose owners derived income from selling government-allocated, controlled-price raw materials on the black market. Tamilnadu, however, is more prosperous than Orissa, and its small industries participate in a national economy of which Orissa is only marginally a part. A much larger proportion of small industries in Tamilnadu, and in our sample, were at the upper end of the small-scale investment range than in Orissa. Seventeen (22 per cent) had investments of Rs. 300,000 or more, as compared with 3 in Orissa (6 per cent).

Tamilnadu firms used more advanced technologies to manufacture products required in the complex economy of a mechanized world. India's largest manufacturer of surveying instruments in 1975 was a Tamilnadu small-scale industry. So was one of the largest producers of precision ball bearings. Electronic counting and sorting equipment, plastic parts for a variety of uses from pens to automobile timing gears, small appliances, motion picture projectors, additives for livestock feed, antennae for India's space program, bifocal lenses for eyeglasses, wheels and pulleys for railway cars, and fuses for telephone equipment were all manufactured by people in our Tamilnadu sample. These manufacturers were sophisticated as well as prosperous businessmen. Well educated or not, they had a level of analytic detachment and well developed managerial skill absent in most of our Orissa group.

Even the manufacturers of basic consumer goods like those that dominated Orissa's small-scale output participated in and oriented themselves toward a larger economic and social network. One respondent manufactured hair oil, an indigenous consumer good comparable to the *gurakhu* manufactured in Orissa. This manufacturer used a generations-old formula in mixing the ingredients for his product; but his mixers were electrically driven, and his vats were stainless steel. He advertised his product and sold to a mass market. After suffering a stroke, he turned company operations over to his daughter. She was a lawyer and served on the all-India Board of Film Censors. Two of his sons earned doctorates in the United States. He was the only professed atheist in the entire sample.

A manufacturer of wooden boats sold his product to the navy and to various port trusts throughout South India. He brought his workers, boat builders by family tradition, as a team from their home state of Kerala. Christians, they spent eleven months a year plying their craft in the factory, returning home for the Christmas holidays.

Most of the successful entrepreneurs in our Tamilnadu sample came from wealthy families. While several were the first in their families to become manufacturers, they were not self-made men who began humbly and flourished by exploiting new opportunities. Sixteen of the respondents' fathers were traders; fathers of 12 were engaged in larger-scale manufacture; fathers of 9 were government servants. Approximately half of the respondents came from families that already participated in the modern economic and political sector, or had a long business history in the non-modern sector.

Small-scale industries, then, were seen as a new opportunity for those who were already in the higher income brackets. They seized the chance to branch out, increase their prosperity, and diversify. By diversifying, they could offset changes in the fortunes of their original businesses that might otherwise result from new government policies, and they could take advantage of the incentives offered to small industries.

Sometimes those incentives were used in ways not envisioned by the planners. Eight respondents, for example, owned enterprises bought for them by their fathers. Concerned about such threats as nationalization of industry, limits on personal wealth, or lowered ceilings on landholding, parents set up small firms for their children as a way to spread their wealth while camouflaging it. These 8 individuals were the offspring of some of the wealthiest families in the state.

Three small firms in our Tamilnadu sample were dummy corporations embedded in existing large companies. To obtain subsidized raw materials, low-interest loans, or price preferences, these small companies had been established as offshoots and given new names. It was impossible to differentiate them from the parent company by physical plant or product. The only difference was that the presidents of these companies did not have the same names as the presidents of the parent companies. Another type of dummy corporation also existed only in name, but differed from the "embedded" companies in that they did not manufacture anything. At least two companies in our sample and possibly as many as four were of this type. Their owners maintained an industry facade solely to obtain raw materials at controlled prices for resale on the black market.

Two other types of firm also existed for reasons unintended by the small-scale industries program. Our sample contained one of each. The first was the wholly-owned subsidiary of a national corporation. It manufactured the same parts for the company's product as the parent company did. It was intentionally kept small, with no more than 7 workers, and physically separate. Hence it was not required to allow union representation of workers, nor was it subject to Factory Act legislation specifying working conditions and requiring employer contributions to welfare and pension funds. This strategy reduced production costs and made the small factory immune from labor disputes in the parent company, so that some production could continue even in the face of a strike.

A related tactic with similar aims was for family members to operate two or more different companies within the same physical facility. Each factory could then have only seven employees, keep income small enough so that taxes were limited, and avoid union and Factory Act requirements. Except that each had its own set of books, the two companies were virtually indistinguishable, manufacturing the same products on the same machines in the same space.

Most of the more prosperous firms, then, were founded by people with substantial business experience, wealth, or a combination of the two. Among this most prosperous group, however, were individuals who had neither business nor industrial backgrounds. Although they were well-educated and middle class, entering business was a new kind of experience for them, one that generated interesting conflicts. Noteworthy here are the Brahmins. They belonged to the caste and community groups most heavily represented in our Tamilnadu sample. Eight of the 9 were first generation businessmen. Because of their tradition of literacy, they have a history of employment in higher education, law, and the civil service. Nowadays, however, because of the increasing power of non-Brahmin groups, who are anti-Brahmin in sentiment, it has become difficult for Brahmins to maintain their former access to positions in professional schools and in government. Consequently, they have turned to the private sector—often, because of their inexperience or lack of capital, to small-scale industries.

Although these respondents were remarkably successful, they complained more about their problems than did others: first, because they had to learn the methods of running a firm that others from business backgrounds had learned almost by osmosis from their families; second, they seemed to feel a need to reconcile business ethics with personal morality. Finally, they had to make their way in the face of familial attitudes hostile to careers in industry.

One of our prosperous respondents reported how his family lagged behind, as he, working long hours at his business, grew as an industrialist.

People here—even my father-in-law, who is a very rich man—didn't appreciate the work I am doing. The location of the factory in Madras was started for two reasons: (1) industrial peace; (2) to have some material support, or at least moral support, from my father-in-law. In that I was wrong. His attitude is, money should be counted every day. He asks me, 'How much bank balance do you have?' I say none. But I have hard work and good will. I have the means with me. If he asks me if I can raise Rs. 20 thousand? Yes, I can; I have my machines, they are my investment. But he is not impressed by that.

This reflects not only a lack of familial support, but also an orientation that one might call the trader attitude, focusing as it does on a concern for financial liquidity. Interestingly enough, the caviling father-in-law was a lawyer. His business, like that of most professionals, required little investment; traders, likewise, realize returns on their investment quickly and can speedily convert their assets into cash if necessary. Manufacturing, by contrast, is a complicated process in which more things can go wrong—labor problems, raw material and power shortages, government regulations— and even when they go right, the return on investment is much longer in coming than it is in trade or the professions. Those in our sample who came from trading rather than manufacturing families often felt frustrated with the manufacturing process. Many reported that they wished to give up manufacturing and return to trading or do something else. Several did. One even shed his simple clothes, had his hair styled, and became a film producer. Others both manufactured one product and held the distributorship (agency) for the same or similar products—their view being that they made greater profits with less risk, and substantially less nuisance.

Some of the younger respondents from trading families, by contrast, emphasized the positive side to manufacturing. "We are making something, . . . not simply taking something out. We are adding to the wealth of our country."

A focus on the modern industries may again lead us astray when considering the small-scale sector in Tamilnadu, for some adapted traditional products, similar to those we saw in Orissa. Two manufacturers in Tamilnadu almost directly paralleled Orissa manufacturers in their application of modern marketing to indigenous products: a manufacturer and distributor of scented and spiced betel nut, and the manufacturer of hair oil.

Spiced and scented betel nut is a traditional product, but this respondent used modern packaging, advertising, and unusual combinations of flavors to increase demand for his product. Doing an acknowledged business of Rs. 750,000 per year, he was an aggressive marketer, so much so that, thinking we had come to

India looking for a manufacturer of his product so that we might distribute it in America, he not only plied us with elaborate food, but loaded us down with a case of samples of his product despite our protestations that we were what we said we were. There are several levels of sophistication here. That he perceived the potential of an American market showed an awareness of the world. Yet, the flavor of the dry, slightly bitter betel nut—chewed as compulsively by many Indians as cigarettes are smoked by some Americans—is far from any standard American taste. That masses of Americans were longing to have high quality Indian betel confections was, consequently, a serious misperception.

We have seen that the most prosperous among Tamilnadu's small-scale industrialists sprang from what could be called upper-middle-class|backgrounds. Small-scale industries were not, for this group, the vehicle to generate new wealth. Instead, they provided new opportunities to protect wealth already acquired and the social position that goes with it.

Others, by contrast, did have firms that provided a satisfactory source of income, and a route for upward mobility. At the bottom of this group was an uneducated young man who employed six workers in the manufacture of trunks and utensils. Working side by side with them, he netted about Rs. 500 a month, a sum realized by selling both manufactured items and part of his raw material allocation (which, in fact, was sold for him through a network before he ever saw it: he received his payment, minus bribes and transportation costs). This was substantially more than he would earn working for somebody else. Each year since starting his business, he earned more than he had the previous year. At the time we interviewed him, he was hesitantly considering investing in machinery. Although he was uncertain he could get enough raw materials at favorable prices to feed the machinery, he was investigating. Youthful, confident, and cheerful about his future prospects, he was quite different from his fellow workers in Tamilnadu and from the dolorous fellows in similar positions in Orissa.

A manufacturer of mosaic tile also fit into this category. Reporting annual gross revenues of Rs. 100,000, almost certainly an underestimate, and a net profit to himself of about Rs. 20,000, he earned as much as a middle-level civil servant. A scheduled-caste person, his father was a fisherman. He had come far, and was confident and proud. Another man manufactured refrigeration boxes, assembling small compressors and attaching them to chambers made from steel sheets. He invested his profits in land in

Madras, on which he was running a small restaurant and auto repair business, his refrigeration activities having diminished in importance by the time we interviewed him. Another respondent began as a day-labor metal bender. He and his son operated a company whose technology was still metalbending, but for office furniture rather than utensils. Black market and legitimate business activities produced an income for him, he said, comparable to that of the tile maker. Still another had a highly mechanized utensil business. That business, which he set up for his younger brother, was still expanding. If they could ever purchase adequate supplies of raw materials, it would become profitable. His father had a low status occupation, dealing in hides and skins. A candy manufacturer admitted to profits of Rs. 2,000 a month (equal to the pay of a high civil servant); he planned to sell his business and retire to his village, where he had purchased land. Although some members of the wealthy families had substantial business achievements to their credit, this group represented those from humble origins who defined themselves as making good, despite what in some cases might seem to be a modest income.

Summary

Madras, like many major cities, exhibited a wide range of small industries, running the gamut from sophisticated modern ones tied to national and international corporations to metal workers hammering out tubs and buckets. We observed different kinds of modern manufacturers. Many of the most prosperous firms were tied to preexisting familial prosperity, often established to provide occupational opportunity for a relative, or to take advantage of economic incentives made available by the Indian government. The prosperous businessmen were well educated and cosmopolitan in outlook.

Below the top level were firms that provided their owners with what they defined as a substantial income in view of their original expectation. Others came to the new industrial class from Brahmin professional and civil servant groups.

CHAPTER SEVEN

ENTREPRENEURIAL PROFILES: PUNJAB

Punjab is India's most prosperous state and is in many ways like no other. To begin with, it is dominated by followers of the Sikh religion; its men—tall, bearded and turbaned—are physically unlike the peoples of the South. Their behaviour is characterized by a rough vitality. If one discounts their striking appearance, Punjabis call to mind some of the classic descriptions of frontier Americans, particularly those of de Tocqueville, Mrs. Trollope and Dickens. Sikhs appear both fierce and rustic. Farmers come into town carrying rifles—some long-barreled and quite archaic—to be used in quarrels over land and women. Drunken brawls (although Sikhs should in principle abjure alcohol) are not uncommon, and the highly refined manners that characterize some other parts of India are absent. Mrs. Trollope's comments on the coarseness of American manners are apposite here: non-Punjabi Indians describe Punjabi manners with similar disapproval. Discussions among Punjabi businessmen about fortunes being made and lost have the frenetic quality that both de Tocqueville (with admiration) and Dickens (with disapproval) observed in the United States in the mid-nineteenth century.

As was also true in that period in America, Punjab's towns were growing rapidly at the times of our visits, and public amenities were not keeping pace. Ludhiana's population—400,000 in 1971—had doubled with each decennial census since Independence. Jullundur, the state's second largest town, has grown almost as fast. The crowded bazaars, open drains, absence of parkland, inadequate internal transportation, and miles of unpaved roads all contributed to public squalor and discomfort, and contrasted with available amenities, from burgeoning "model towns" (the Indian name for new urban middle-class neighborhoods) to shops filled with arrays of attractive merchandise. Signs of prosperity were everywhere.

Punjabis owned most of the tractors in India. Tractors also served prosperous farmers as family cars, crowding the roads and causing traffic jams as family members and friends perched on the tractor's high rear fenders or in wagons drawn behind them. Overfilled trucks, crowded intertown buses, small three-wheeled vehicles so heavily laden that the lone front wheel might collapse, all fought for their share of the road. The heavy vehicular traffic was augmented by the ubiquitous bullock carts and bicycles.

The state's comparative wealth meant that manufactured goods—bicycles, flashlights, and transistor radios, for example—were widely available and widely owned. Even the numerous restaurants, running the gamut from deluxe air-conditioned establishments to open-front stalls with a few simmering pots to fast food carts piled high with potato balls, sweet hot chickpeas, and onion, ginger, and garlic relishes, connoted unusual prosperity and extraordinary gusto.

Punjabis flourish economically not only in Punjab, but throughout India. Explaining their singular success is an intellectual problem that has perplexed both Indians and visiting foreigners. Punjab is India's granary, with the highest wheat yields in the nation. Located on a broad, fertile plain, Punjab's natural water resources were augmented when the British built an elaborate canal system in the nineteenth century. By itself, this does not explain Punjab's success, since other parts of India have even more fertile land. What distinguishes Punjab, in this and other regards, is its relentless exploitation of available resources. Punjabis have, for example, made the most extensive use of modern agricultural technology. There are more tractors, tube wells, and mechanical threshers in Punjab than in any other Indian state. Punjabis were the first to plant seeds of high-yielding varieties of wheat, and the first to adopt new planting techniques. Punjabis were, historically, mechanically innovative as well. Many of our small-scale industrialists came from families of village artisans who built Persian wheels and other preindustrial mechanical agricultural equipment.

The most striking characteristic of small industries in Punjab was the high level of specialization in production. Ludhiana concentrated on knitted woolen items: sweaters, socks, and scarves; woven cotton textiles; bicycles and bicycle parts; sewing machine parts; automobile parts; and machine tools. Jullundur specialized in printing and printing goods, water pipes and bathroom fixtures, and sporting goods. Nearby Batala specialized in foundries. The first two cities are part of an industrial belt that runs from Khanna through Ludhiana to Jullundur. Intervening cities also specialize. Goraya, a town of 6,000 between Ludhiana and Jullundur, had nine agricultural machinery factories at the time of the study. Similar industries are located next to each other, generating high densities of related industries, which in turn generate specialized labor forces, rapid communication of information, and great interdependence. In addition, this centralization of industry by type makes it possible for buyers to come to a city, assured that desired purchases can be made in a small area.

Neighborhoods within towns also specialize. In Basti Nau in Jullundur city, more than a hundred sporting goods manufacturers are clustered together, producing cricket bats and balls, badminton rackets and shuttlecocks, table tennis rackets and nets, carrom boards, and other sports equipment. Basti Nau (literally, "new neighborhood") is special because its residents came originally from Sailkot, in what is now Pakistan and migrated to India together after Partition. Orissa and Tamilnadu have specialized markets where particular goods are sold, but factories producing those goods are not located together. In Tamilnadu, the government had a program to create functional industrial estates—that is, to generate a setting similar to that which grew organically in Punjab—but it was not very successful.

Area specialization is carried to an extreme in Ludhiana. In 1965, 1,600 knitted goods and staple cloth factories were registered as small-scale industries there, representing perhaps one-half to two-thirds of all such industries in the city. Most of them huddle together along the dark, narrow, winding lanes of the old quarter. Many are located in homes.

The textile industry is highly integrated, and because specialization is so refined, one can enter it at any level. For a minuscule investment—about Rs. 300 in the 1970s—one could buy a knitting machine to make socks, gloves, or sleeves. One did not need a factory building, since one could put it in one's home. One did not need working capital, since other manufacturers supplied raw materials to be fabricated into finished goods. Such companies paid only for the owner's labor (or that of his wife or children), a twentieth century equivalent of the putting-out system.

Alternatively, one might buy a machine to manufacture sweater bodies; these cost about Rs. 2,500. Other people will sew sleeves onto bodies, make labels, and sew the labels onto the sweaters. In short, these industries exemplify the advantages of specialization and interdependence. In the fall and early winter, the area is a scene of almost frenzied activity. Skeins of freshly dyed wool are everywhere, hanging out in the sun to dry. The knitting machines and cloth looms run night and day, each producing a distinctive noise. Carts laden with wool and sweaters in various stages of manufacture crowd the narrow streets, as do individuals purposefully hurrying to negotiate deals. Itinerant Tibetan peddlers, packs on their backs or shoulders, prowl the streets buying up stock to sell all over India (sometimes as genuine hand-knit Tibetan sweaters). The feeling of purposeful busyness, of time as money, is reminiscent of New York's garment district.

Other sections of Ludhiana are highly specialized. Reaching out in most directions from the central city are industrial estates and industrial areas, acre after acre of small, newly constructed sheds whose numbering system defies one to find a particular factory. Unlike the landscaped Guindy in Madras, unlike even the industrial estate near Cuttack, the buildings here, because of the speed of construction, rest in a sea of mud during the rainy season and sit under clouds of dust the rest of the year. Roads are unpaved and rutted. Most of the bicycle-parts manufacturers and bicycle assemblers were located in Industrial Area B, where individual firms manufacture cycle fenders, seat pillars, seats, cranks, pedals, freewheels, handlebars, and even specialized nuts and bolts for bicycles. Just as in the old city one finds carts heaped with sweater parts, here carts are piled high with bicycle seats, pedals, and handlebars.

Similarly, other manufacturers follow the same pattern of minute specialization and interdependence. Most machine tool manufacturers were located together along the Grand Trunk Road; most textile machinery manufacturers and wool processors were near each other in Industrial Area A.

After a period of rapid expansion, aided by a seller's market that often accepted inferior goods, many of these businesses were enormously profitable—the number of new houses in Ludhiana attests to that—and black-market activities augmented their profitability. By 1971, supply had caught up to demand, and once-huge profit margins were being squeezed by the high cost of black-market raw materials and pricing pressures from competitors. Respondents had predicted a shakeout among the 1,324 cycle parts manufacturers of Ludhiana as their costs for raw materials approached their retail prices, but by 1975, the mood had changed dramatically. Raw materials prices had been pushed down by a combination of forces stemming from the state of emergency declared by Mrs. Gandhi. These forces included no-strike legislation, one effect of which was to increase production at government steel mills; another was a recession caused by the government's avid pursuit of black-market money.

Punjabi cycle parts manufacturers who in 1971 were nibbling at the fringes of the export market had by 1975 entered it enthusiastically. One manufacturer's entire output was being sold abroad, principally to the countries of southeast Asia. Others had entered new cycle-parts lines, sometimes constructing new facilities for their manufacture. One company had previously manufactured seat pillars—bars that go under bicycle seats to give them rigidity. The company had moved to a technologically more sophisticated level with a product very much more in demand—the bottom bracket of the bicycle, where the frame joins together and holds the crank. This company reported its production was inadequate to meet demand. Others, once raw material prices had declined, found they could be competitive and make reasonable profits once again. Still others had begun manufacturing entirely new product lines. Most dramatic among those was one making hand tools for the export market. Sweater manufacturers, too, had discovered the export market. Manufacturers in Ludhiana were selling bulk orders directly to Eastern European countries. Manufacturers in our small sample sold more than $100,000 worth of sweaters to the Soviet Union and Czechoslovakia in 1974. The knitted goods industry played a large role in shaping Ludhiana's industry and its distinctive attributes. This structure is not unique in India, but it accounts in part for the orderly growth of industry and the many trained people in the area.

The knitted goods firms make up a modern, but old, industry. It began before the turn of the century and grew very gradually. This organic growth contrasts with attempts, in many parts of India, to set up industries that would be fully developed from their inception. Some succeed; others do not.

Initially, sweaters were made with machines imported from England. These machines needed repairs, however, and as people learned to fix the machines, a pool of technically proficient repairmen developed. By the 1920s, these repairmen were making their own machines, defying patent infringement lawsuits brought by the British. The long-range outcome was the orderly growth, as increasing numbers of trained workers became available, of machine-based industry. Producing and maintaining textile machinery required and generated the skills necessary to manufacture other goods. Significantly, each succeeding industry also grew slowly and steadily. The high degree of specialization that followed made it possible for people with limited capital to enter the emerging industries.

Who were the manufacturers in Ludhiana and Jullundur? To begin with, as in Tamilnadu, many manufacturers came from the commercial families that historically provided many of Punjab's businessmen. The biggest knitting factories in the small-scale sector were owned by families who also owned the large mills in the area: Jains, Aggarwals, and Khatris. The sewing machine assembly and distribution business was likewise dominated by a single commercial caste, the Aroras.

In Jullundur, apart from the sporting goods industry, many small industries were set up by the big commercial families. They sought to provide income for a younger brother or son, a pattern also evident in Tamilnadu. Many of these manufacturers expressed the same ambivalence as did their counterparts in Tamilnadu: it takes too long to realize profits from manufacturing, and the lack of liquidity while capital is invested without yielding a return makes investors uncomfortable.

About 40 per cent of our respondents were refugees from the area that became Pakistan after Partition. They constituted about one-third of the subsample in Ludhiana and slightly more than one-half in Jullundur. The refugees' performance, measured in output and investment, was about the same as that of the nonrefugees, although they were more likely to come from business backgrounds than were the natives.

Just as Tamilnadu had a growing industrial class of Brahmins, and Orissa had one of outsiders who dominated that state's industries, there was a special industrial class in Ludhiana: the Ramgarhia Sikhs. Ramgarhias are an artisan community—one hesitates to say caste—heavily concentrated in Ludhiana. Members of the group specialize in working with machinery—so much so, that Ludhiana residents believe that Ramgarhias have inborn mechanical skills. As a group, they were numerically dominant in almost all Ludhiana's small-parts manufacture: bicycle parts, sewing machine parts, automobile parts, and machine tools. Many of them intermarried; and many of them, perhaps following the other commercial classes, had become vegetarian, an unusual pattern for Sikhs, but a common one for many business communities—Jains, Gujarati Banias, Marwaris—elsewhere in India.

Together with the belief that Ramgarhias are uncannily skillful with machinery goes the belief—held by those both in and out of the community—that Ramgarhias cannot do well in school. In the late nineteenth century, Ramgarhia uplift societies bemoaned this fact in their newspapers, and Ramgarhias still bemoan it today. Many children of prosperous Ramgarhia families had not gone past the eighth grade; many within the community were becoming concerned that, without more education, they would be unable to make the transition from being worker-owners and operators of their businesses to being well-educated owner-managers. Like the poorer small industrialists in Madras, many hired non-family, non-community members to keep their books, do their correspondence, and deal with clerical matters. Having to rely on outsiders, however, made them nervous, for they were uncertain that such employees could be trusted. A few families had, in fact, made the transition, among them, the largest automobile-parts manufacturer in Ludhiana at the time of the study. Nonetheless, Ramgarhias feared that the monied commercial classes would come to dominate their industries through having more capital and the superior administrative skills that higher levels of schooling can provide

The limited education and lack of tradition of family wealth among machine-tool industrialists in Ludhiana gave their style a distinct flavor. In Tamilnadu, the owner of a factory was likely to be found behind a desk, wearing whites, administering the firm but having little first-hand knowledge of machines. The owner of a small Punjab factory, by contrast, was likely to be found under a machine, effecting some repair. The labor force in these factories often consisted of a few brothers and sons, with supplemental low-wage migrant workers from nearby Uttar Pradesh. A Ramgarhia boss could operate a lathe at least as well as any of his workers. He and others designed machines after looking at pictures of them. (Our respondent in Orissa who designed a cold storage and ice plant and built it with his brothers was actually an "immigrant" Ramgarhia.)

Ramgarhias also had an acute sense of the limitations of what they could produce. They did not sound quite like some of the more heroic enterprisers of the entrepreneurial literature. "My product is not very good now," many told us. "But it was worse before, and it will get better as my machinery gets better and we are able to work with more precision." Tamilnadu manufacturers spent substantially more time telling us about the fine quality of their goods as compared to the Punjabis'. Historically, their products had a reputation for high quality and Punjabi products a reputation for low price. The prevailing sellers' market for manufactured goods meant, in Punjab, that one made what one could, sold it for what he could get, and reinvested. One's product improved, one's prices went up, and one's sophistication rose with the market—to the extent that Punjab was closing the quality gap between its products and those of Tamilnadu. One man who has used the products of Punjabi small industry, himself a resident of Ludhiana, reported that in the mid-1960s, when he needed a part, he ordered four or five to be sure of getting one that approximated the required dimensions. An American working nearby had a similar report. Between 1965 and 1970, quality improved dramatically and by 1975, it was high enough to compete in world markets. More good machinery was available and people had more money to buy it.

Also in contradistinction to the descriptions in the entrepreneurship literature, and to the businessmen Max Weber admired in India, these men, far from being ascetic, were conspicuous consumers of many personal goods. Elaborately tiled new houses, pastel-colored lavatories, stereo sets, and television (despite the lack at that time of adequate programming and poor reception) were quickly acquired with the new wealth.

While it was hard to collect systematic data on the question, some portion of government loans to small industrialists in Punjab often went into house construction and to equipment; this diversion of funds was sometimes justified by locating the house next to the factory.

Some of this zealous acquisition of material goods resulted from the need to dispose of black money, but also stemmed in part from the idea of conspicuous consumption as an index of family status. Immigrant Punjabis in London sent money home for elegant houses to be constructed in their villages. In short, the Punjabis are unusually hard and able workers whose efforts have earned them wealth. Frugal living and self-abnegation—notwithstanding the vegetarianism—are not, however, part of the model.

Refugees from Pakistan have played a role in the developments we are describing, although not as central a role in Punjab's economic growth as is sometimes claimed. The Ramgarhias, so important to the development of Ludhiana, were local people from nearby villages in the district. A few held jobs in Lahore at the time of Partition, at which time they returned to Ludhiana, but most were local people who left home.

At the time of our study, there were rumors that non-Sikh businessmen were being driven from Punjab following the state's most recent partition, into Punjab and Haryana. Three respondents in our sample of 41 non-Sikhs supported this. Two had opened factories in other states, one in Haryana and one in Uttar Pradesh. One of the factories was a branch of the existing industry, the other manufactured an entirely unrelated product line. The third respondent was a printer. Not knowing the Gurmukhi script used in writing Punjabi, and not owning Gurmukhi type fonts, his business declined by 80 per cent at the creation of a more heavily Sikh Punjab. He had been trying to sell his printing presses ever since.

In our discussions of Orissa and Tamilnadu, we have shown how the concepts "traditional" and "modern" fail adequately to characterize reality. Each implies complexes of values, attitudes, and behaviors that often fail to vary together in real life. A manufacturer in Ludhiana known as Guruji (revered teacher) exemplifies the use of traditional forms in promoting the dispersion of modern techniques. Guruji operated the "Women's Hosiery Company" which made the body part of sweaters. He described the process:

> We collect raw materials from a manufacturer, make the sweater parts, and give them back. I do not have enough money to buy my own raw materials. For this we get one rupee per kilogram. In one day I manufacture fifty to sixty kilos. Unfortunately, the season is only five to six months. Each year I pick one man to work with me as an apprentice, after examining him to ascertain his interest and his diligence, but I only take one. I pay him Rs. 150 per month. Many parents bring their sons. He is then well trained and able to go out and take a job for a substantially large sum of money—about Rs. 500 per month to start. I am childless. I have raised one niece who is in college in New Delhi. But all of my apprentices are my children, and they visit me regularly.

Guruji was an unambitious, pious man who lived simply and thought philosophically. He also knew more about the operation of knitting machines than any other person we met in Ludhiana. His house was both a source of religious guidance and a clearing-house for the knitting machine operators in the center of the knitting industry in the old part of town.

As the interview progressed and the day wore on, Guruji's

"children" began to drift in. The latter part of our visit included sitting in on an intense, spirited discussion of various aspects of the knitting business: which manufacturers had gotten big contracts with whom that day and would therefore be hiring; how to adjust the machine's tension for the thread of a new synthetic yarn; how to set up machines for a new kind of weave that made cotton and rayon feel like wool (Guruji disapproved of this, but knew every detail of the process); and how to set up the machines to produce a new pattern that, it was predicted, would take the market by storm. On another day, the scene looked the same, but the quality of talk was astonishing: Indian politics, world politics, the textile industry, and international cricket matches were discussed by a group whose mean education was below the completion of high school. Guruji himself had never attended school.

Guruji was a local figure of repute. Rickshaw pullers had never heard of the Woman's Hosiery Company and could not find his factory; but they had all heard of Guruji and could locate his house (which was, of course, also the site of his factory), although it was located down a narrow back alley. They often refused payment for the ride, since Guruji himself, so we were told, gave money from his modest income to others more in need than himself.

Guruji, then, was the archetype of the traditional respected man: wise, simple, and austere in habits, kind and gentle in disposition, surrounded by disciples. Yet in addition to discoursing on holy or esoteric subjects, he talked about knitting machines and the knitting industry. He was the center of an information network, dispensing advice on economic opportunities for his disciples and disseminating knowledge to members of the knitting industry. A Brahmin, Guruji as teacher filled a traditional caste-related role. His knitting machine, however, was one of the most modern available in Ludhiana.

Summary

Punjab has been characterized by very rapid growth in the small-scale sector, a growth shared by its towns. Businesses were highly concentrated in towns and in specific neighborhoods within the towns. This led to high levels of interdependence, and helped make possible low entry costs for anyone trying to start a business. As in the other states, many firms were run by or connected to families who had already amassed wealth in commerce and whose heritage included a tradition in trade. The notable exception to this was the Ramgarhia Sikh community of artisans who controlled most of the machining occupations in Ludhiana.

A dense network of rail and road transportation, the early growth of small interdependent industries, and the traditions of the Ramgarhia Sikhs must all be considered in accounting for Punjab's rapid growth. Migrants from Pakistan contributed both to urban population growth and to the vitality of industry, but did not by themselves account for it.

Punjab in 1971, and again in 1975, was a boom state. This atmosphere contributed to a growth-oriented mentality. People were eager to enter business for themselves in anticipation of making their fortunes. The role of agricultural prosperity in generating industrial prosperity is difficult to assess. Five of the 75 small firms in our sample were directly or indirectly connected with agriculture. Three of them were in a slightly depressed condition during the 1971 boom. We counted all the agricultural products factories we could find in the industrial areas, but there were few; some of them, however, were spectacularly profitable. These included a factory manufacturing a simple threshing machine and an agricultural-sprayer manufacturing company.

Punjab's reliance for its prosperity on national and international markets leads us to believe that there is no simple relationship between the success of small industry and the vigor of the agricultural sector, although each benefits from the presence of the other. The structure of small industry in Punjab, however, was peculiarly well suited to the situation Punjabis faced. The high levels of specialization and interdependence made it possible for an ambitious young man to go into industry with a small investment. If he was part of the right social network, his opportunities to succeed increased greatly. The densities of particular industries reduced the problems small industrialists had in finding raw materials, trained laborers, and markets for their products. Raw materials were at their doorsteps, trained laborers knocked at their doors daily looking for work, and customers came from all over India to seek their products at a centralized location.

CHAPTER EIGHT

THE STATES COMPARED

Our original intention in studying small-scale industries in three states rather than just one was to make comparisons among them that would teach us about the genesis of different problems of small-industrial development in India. Such an exercise, of course, assumed sufficient similarity among the units observed to enable one to isolate important differences and determine the reasons for them. It turned out, however, that the states were so different as to make the value of comparison questionable. To try to learn about the structure of small-scale industries in Punjab by studying Orissa, for example, is something like learning about New York City by studying Appalachia. Orissa, in the small-scale sector at least, seemed almost to be pre-Industrial Revolution, a state of affairs reflected in the orientations that the industrialists brought to their work as well as the problems they faced. In this context, statistics reporting national averages for "the small-scale sector" are misleading at best.

It is remarkable that the qualitative differences could be so great, given the forces at work to produce homogeneity. The Small-Scale Industries Program was a national policy which, though administered independently and with slightly different features and emphases by each state, nonetheless was designed and implemented along fairly uniform lines. The environments in which the industrialists operated were similar. Thus, the constraints imposed by government—the Factory Act, labor laws, the tax structure—as well as problems of obtaining access to raw materials and market, were virtually the same in all three states. Yet, the settings in which these forces operated were so different that the outcomes were dramatically different as well. Simple generalizations that apply to all the states are impossible to make.

One core difference is the density and volume of industrial activity. The enormous concentration of very small industries in Punjab created conditions that, in some respects, resembled the classical perfect market. Because there were many small manufacturers instead of a few large ones, the decisions of any individual manufacturer would not—with the possible exception of a few large sweater manufacturers or wool processors—ramify to affect the entire industry. The high densities, combined with shared locations, also meant that information about manufacturing processes, available raw materials, and markets traveled very fast. Naturally, it did not travel with equal speed in all directions. Particular industries were often dominated by large extended kin or communal networks, and information travels more freely through these than it does outside them.

These densities allow for a very refined division of labor and specialization of function among the firms. This division of labor led both to dramatic interdependence and to the development of support systems essential for small producers. Our Tamilnadu and Orissa respondents often bemoaned the difficulty of having to do everything, from purchasing raw materials to organizing the fabrication to finding buyers for the finished product. In Punjab, one had at hand varied raw materials and finished parts at prices and qualities that were widely known; trained labor and customers—both marketing agents and end-use customers who knew that they could get what they wanted if they came here—were plentiful.

Small firms in Madras, by contrast, depended on a few large firms for the bulk of their sales. A railroad coach manufacturer, a manufacturer of machine tools, an automobile parts manufacturer, a bicycle manufacturer and a tire manufacturer together accounted for a large segment of any small producer's sales. A much higher proportion of manufacturers in Madras than in Ludhiana fabricated metal goods to order, for example, because demand was insufficient to warrant mass production. Each fabricator bid regularly, as specifications were published or announced, on jobs let by the large manufacturers. Hence, the fortunes of any individual enterprise could ride on winning or losing a contract. One fabricator we interviewed in 1971 was struggling along, unable to get the contracts he needed to prosper. Subsequently, he captured one and ultimately a series of contracts for the fabrication and assembly of steel components for India's space program. His fortunes changed dramatically. Conversely, another manufacturer fell from prosperity to near bankruptcy because the purchasing agent of his major customer, a large tire manufacturer, was caught taking bribes in the selection of his company's suppliers—a not uncommon scenario. The customer canceled all of its contracts, leaving the contractors to cope as best they could.

The lower density of industrial concentration also meant that a much greater proportion of manufacturers in Tamilnadu than in Punjab produced finished goods through all the stages of production (18 per cent compared to 6 per cent). Small-scale producers in our Tamilnadu sample manufactured 70 millimeter projectors, surveying instruments, and diesel engines beginning with castings of the components, a procedure almost unthinkable in Punjab, where an assembler would go to the market for most of his parts. In Tamilnadu, one did not gain the advantages of mass production. The volume of sales did not warrant it. Everyone agreed that products from Tamilnadu cost more than their Punjab counterparts. It also used to be said that they were of better quality. By 1975, that perception of difference in quality had become rarer.

M. Panini has compared small manufacturers in Faridabad near New Delhi with manufacturers in Mysore in South India (personal communication) and found similar differences. A South Indian himself, he believes that South Indians do not trust others, and consequently manufacture as much as they can themselves. While this explanation is plausible, it has some problems. First although we hesitate to argue from stereotypes, common wisdom in India would have it the other way. Both north and south Indians in general believe that northerners are not to be trusted and southerners, whatever their other defects (they are thought to be unimaginative and cautious), are. Large business families throughout north India employ southerners to keep their books because of the southerners' supposed trustworthiness. Following Panini, one might argue that the southerners' caution encourages the manufacture of whole products. One cannot be sure that there will be adequate supplies of high-quality parts available on the open market when they are needed.

Another line of argument follows Adam Smith and his successors, noting that the division of labor can succeed only where markets are large enough to sustain it. Perhaps south Indians were cut off from the larger markets of north India, both by the earlier arrival of manufacturing in the north and by the differences of language and culture. Punjabis sell their wares in a much larger market than do the Madrasis, whose products are more limited to the south, particularly to Tamilnadu itself and the adjoining state of Andhra Pradesh.

This argument can be pursued further by examining manufacturing in Orissa.

In Orissa, almost half of the manufacturers produced whole products, but most products, in general, were rudimentary. The market for manufactured goods in Orissa was too small to sustain successful manufacturers who, consequently, had to compete in regional markets to succeed. Efforts to compete nationally failed dramatically. A state-supported attempt to establish a medium-scale automobile battery manufacturer failed so disastrously that even the State Trading Corporation refused to take the product. A government-sponsored effort to manufacture television sets also failed. Supporters had claimed it would upgrade the local people's skills and improve the image of the state as a modern manufacturer; but local people could not afford to purchase the sets, and the local brand had to compete nationally with better|known|and advertised names. This was but one in a series of misguided policies aimed at propelling Orissa into the industrial world.

As we have seen, the major industrial successes of Orissa were in food preparation, where one simply mixed the raw materials, subjected them to some simple processes, packaged the product, and distributed it. The biscuit maker and the *gurakhu* manufacturer both fit into this category. They had an advantage over national competitors in these lines because they appealed to local tastes, and they could get their goods to potential customers while still fresh. They also relied on numerous small-volume sales for their success. In addition, although their investments had become relatively large—around Rs. 750,000—their machinery was primitive (a mechanic in the *gurakhu* factory built all of theirs) and required neither a skilled labor force to operate it, skilled workers to repair it, nor scarce, finely tooled parts. Nowhere in Orissa could one rely on finding high quality raw materials or replacement parts.

If one wished to succeed at higher levels of sophistication in Orissa, he had to import machinery, raw materials, and workers from Calcutta. If he manufactured a sophisticated product, Calcutta was the nearest large potential market as well. In such a setting, the only successes were very large industries with enormous investments, which established colonies within the state and brought equipment, workers, and management from outside. The only successful modern industries in Orissa operated this way. The glass manufacturer used indigenous fire clay; but virtually all of his machinery was imported from the United States, and his workmen fabricated replacement parts when machinery broke. His factory sat in a company town, almost a colony, where he had a labor force that was going into its second generation of working in the factory.

The most dramatic example of an independent colony was the German-built Rourkela steel plant, which was constructed with its own self-sufficient township. It was managed from New Delhi, and almost all of its trained personnel came from outside. Around it some small-scale industries had grown up, most of which supplied the factory with components. The small-scale industrialists were not local people, either. On a tour of Rourkela's small-scale industries in 1975, we met Punjabis, Gujaratis, Marwaris, and others. Our request to meet some Orissan manufacturers did not produce a single one. These small industries, too, were subject to the constraints that Tamilnadu's industries faced, but even more so. Because of Rourkela's geographic isolation, they were wholly dependent on the steel plant for their custom. Planners used to argue that such a pattern of ancillary industries was beneficial to small industries, because the existence of a mother factory would guarantee them orders. The other side of that picture, however, is the utter dependence of the ancillary industry for its survival on orders from the parent. Indeed, one's fate is so closely tied to the moods of a single purchasing agent that industrialists' fortunes rise and fall mercurially.

With access only to such limited or specialized markets, one had to compete nationally if one was to succeed as an industrialist in Orissa. Yet given an inadequate labor force and limited availability of specialized equipment, a whole world had to be brought in for one to succeed. Tamilnadu had a similar set of problems on a more manageable scale. In Madras, we visited a foundry that manufactured high-quality high-pressure valves and elbows for pipes. With an investment of Rs. 20 million, the factory had a German electric arc furnace and European overhead cranes. Special sand for castings was carried by train from India's west coast, and ore was transported over great distances as well. Unlike most of our successful small-scale manufacturers, this large-scale manufacturer did have an all-India market for his scarce product. The same was true of a ball-bearing manufacturer, who had begun in the small-scale sector, but moved into the large scale (with the help of capital from other family-owned enterprises), selling a product for which there was enormous demand in the nationwide market.

Some relevant numbers support this analysis, which concerns itself with the possibilities inherent in the division of labor. We asked respondents to tell us the size of their original investment, size of current investment, total annual sales, and number of employees. We also asked about profits, but found our respondents understandably evasive; Indian income tax was at that time steeply progressive, and most respondents acknowledged underreporting their income for tax purposes. Consequently, we used total sales as a surrogate variable for profits, because of respondents' reluctance to report profits and because of the ambiguity inherent in the concept of profit as applied to a small company. In many cases, respondents reported that their firm showed little or no profit; yet a father and three brothers all drew comfortable salaries, and wrote off as business expenses such items as automobiles that were often used for family as well as business purposes. It does not make sense to call those companies unprofitable. Gross revenue, of course, does not tell us the magnitude of profits—respondents usually reported that profits were somewhere between 10 and 20 per cent of their annual revenue—but it does give us a rough determination of rank order of profitability within similar categories. We weighed the importance of the gross income figure by considering other measures as well: our own assessment of profitability based on our observation of the intensity of activity in the factory (a subjective measure), the life-style of the respondent, and his own report about how he thought his business was doing.

Our third attempt at measuring profitability involved comparing 1971 investment size with original investment size. This was also a crude indicator that assumed more profitable businesses generate larger investments—crude because it is not always true, and does not consider year of founding. It nonetheless related well to the other two. None of these is ideal, but we became increasingly confident of our observations when we returned to these factories after a four-year lapse. After twenty minutes inside of any factory, we were able to tell reliably whether our respondents' business had increased or decreased in the intervening years, and by about how much.

To be sure, there are difficulties with this approach. In 1971, raw materials were in such short supply that many companies overstated their sales to be eligible for an increased allocation of raw materials, which they could then sell in the black market. We found, however, that as our familiarity with Indian factories increased, we could identify those cases readily. In 1975, the availability of raw materials (and, consequently, the reduced motivation to exaggerate sales), and government efforts—successful in the short term—to drive out black-market money, gave us a new perspective.

Comparing 1971 and 1975 investment and gross revenue figures for the three states, a trend is clear. In 1971, mean gross income for our Tamilnadu respondents was Rs. 265,507 on an investment in plant and equipment of Rs. 223,000, for an investment-to-gross index of .84. By contrast, the average gross income in Punjab was Rs. 319,217 on an investment of only Rs. 196,620, for an investment-to-gross index of .61. This means that the Punjabis produced 30 per cent more per rupee of investment than did the Tamilnadu group. The Orissan investment-to-gross index was similar to Tamilnadu's, .81.

The Punjabis employed more workers per rupee invested: there was one worker for every Rs. 9,870 invested, as compared to one per Rs. 12,380 in Tamilnadu. Here the Orissans were more like the Punjabis, with one worker per Rs. 9,200 investment. Punjabis not only got more out of their capital, they got more out of their workers as well. Each worker produced Rs. 1,645 of sales in Punjab as compared to only Rs. 1,475 for Tamilnadu and Rs. 1,139 for Orissa. In short, the Punjabis had both more productive capital and more productive workers than the manufacturers in the other states.

Although our data are not strictly comparable (we interviewed only the more prosperous half of our respondents in 1975), the Punjabis surpassed the Tamilnadu group in total average investment by 1975. Punjabis reported a mean increase in investment between 1972 and 1975 of Rs. 128,091, while the Tamilnadu respondents reported an increased investment of Rs. 96,285. Industries in Orissa increased their investment an average of Rs. 20,330 in the same period.

Eighty-eight per cent of the Punjabis in our 1975 sample, but just under half of the Orissa and Tamilnadu samples, reported having made major investments between 1972 and 1975. More dramatic than simple magnitude differences distinguishing the Punjabis from the others is that the Punjabis reported investing in machinery whether or not their industries were profitable in the intervening period. One-third of the Punjabis said they invested money in a declining business situation, in contrast to 6 per cent of the Tamilnadu sample and none of the Orissa group. When drought brought massive power cuts, almost all of the Punjabis bought diesel generators so that production could continue; almost none of the Madrasis did. "If you are not making profits, how can you invest?" they asked. The Punjabis' willingness to take risks, to invest to improve or alter your [product in the face of business decline, is a dramatic difference.

In 1971, we noticed that although the Punjabis and the Madrasis used similar quality machines to produce their goods, the Madrasis seemed to turn out a higher quality finished product. They themselves said that they produced better quality goods than did the Punjabis; that was why they had to charge more for them. Certainly, workers filing off imperfections and improving tolerances in finished goods were a common sight in the Madras factories. The Punjabis were not so careful. In 1975, work in Tamilnadu was still carried on much as it had been in 1971. In Punjab, however, the lower quality machines of 1971 had been replaced by machines that automatically produced unburred, high tolerance products.

The Punjabis did not surpass the Tamilnadu group by using low-wage labor; indeed, the Punjabis paid their workers up to twice as much as the Madrasis did. Nor was the difference the result of heavier investment in obsolete capital equipment in the older area that might have permitted the newer one to leapfrog over it with the latest technology. It has been argued that the United States overtook England as an industrial power in part through its willingness to manufacture goods over a greater quality range than did the British; consequently, the United States won markets away from the British and, by offering lower priced (though also lower quality) merchandise, it could expand existing markets. This describes the situation of Punjab vis-a-vis Tamilnadu nicely. In 1975, the Madrasis continued to work with the same machines. The Punjabis had replaced their original machines with new ones of better quality that were faster, required less careful supervision (and consequently less labor), and, most importantly, were far more accurate. The Tamilnadu manufacturers were losing any advantage they might have had. The Punjabis, faced with a recession at home, had upgraded their products enough to enter international markets. Manufacturers of sweaters, small hand tools, bicycle parts, and cylindrical grinders were exporting their products by 1975, and they were doing so in volumes that, set against average local sales, were truly staggering. A major sweater manufacturer (but still small scale) sold Rs. 7 million worth of sweaters abroad; a tiny sweater manufacturer sold Rs. 100,000 worth through a subcontract. A bicycle freewheel manufacturer (no longer small scale) had exported Rs. 10 million worth of parts, as had another cycle-parts manufacturer. The manufacturer of cylindrical grinders had sold 11 machines abroad, each machine selling for Rs. 40,000 to Rs. 50,000.

Against this growth in Punjab, both the Tamilnadu group and the Orissans were standing still. In part, this resulted from Punjabi attitudes toward investment and toward spending in general. Tamilians do not live ostentatiously. Punjabis are, by contrast, conspicuous consumers. One businessman in our Tamilnadu sample, a Punjabi by birth, articulated this difference clearly: "How can you make money off these people? They do not spend. If you see a man carrying a fountain pen and comment on it, he will tell you that it was his grandfather's and it has given good service. He has no interest in having the latest thing or some new thing." The same caution that leads to a reluctance to spend on new things creates both sluggish markets and entrepreneurial reluctance. The point here is that some ascetics in India may be shrewd, risk-taking investors—such as some of the Jains singled out by Weber (who may not in fact be reinvesting as the modern Punjabis do). Other ascetics pursue wealth but are reluctant to reinvest, except in gold and precious jewelry. Punjabis find the resources both to spend conspicuously and to reinvest in their businesses. This supports the point that many different kinds of people can be entrepreneurs, and the kind who succeeded—or at least are alleged to have succeeded—in the West are but one of an array of styles compatible with success.

The Tamilnadu group was simply disinclined to take risks. Only in Madras did people talk consistently about the desirability of guaranteed profit. We asked all respondents:

Suppose you were manufacturing a product and you had no marketing arrangements for it. You could do one of two things: either (a) obtain a contract for the sale of your total product output, at a very low rate of profit per unit, or (b) compete in the open market, with the possibility of making a much higher profit per unit but with no guarantee about the volume of your sales. Which of these alternatives would you choose?

Seventy per cent of the Madrasis (and of the Orissans as well) chose the safe, lower-profit option. Only 40 per cent of the Punjabis made the same choice. A substantial proportion of the remaining 60 per cent of the Punjabis were almost scornful that one might take the low-profit, low-risk route. Too, many of those who preferred to sell on the open market expressed the fear that if one relied on a single large customer, that customer would have excessive power and, ultimately, could beat their prices down further, consequently reducing their profits. By contrast, Madrasis spoke enthusiastically of the possibility of becoming ancillary to a large corporation, as this would make doing business a sure thing.

As befits individuals who entered their industries with substantially higher initial investments than the others, and who also come from one of the most highly educated states in India, the Tamilnadu respondents were substantially better educated than their counterparts in the other states. Only 17 per cent of them had ended their schooling with a high school education or less, as compared to 72 per cent of the Punjabis and 64 per cent of the Orissans. The differences are not so dramatic at the other end. In Madras, 26 per cent had college degrees, as compared to 19 per cent of the Punjabis and 17 per cent of the Orissans. Interesting here, however, is the similarity in educational levels between the Orissans and the Punjabis. Both enter the industrial world with little education or financial resources; yet the Punjabis subsequently make something of their efforts while the Orissans do not.

In addition to their higher levels of education, the Tamilnadu respondents have had a broader level of exposure to the world outside of India than have either the Punjabis or the Orissans. Thirteen per cent have studied abroad or traveled extensively, as compared to 4 per cent of the Punjabis and 2 per cent of the Orissans. According to Inkeles and Lerner, education and cosmopolitanism are strong correlates of modernization; yet these do not seem in our cases to conduce either to effectiveness in or commitment to industry as a career.

The differences between the Tamilnadu group and the Punjabis in effectiveness and commitment extended to their attitudes toward those who participate in industry. We have two independent ways of measuring this. First, we asked respondents what their children's occupations were. For those who did not have children old enough to be employed, we asked what their aspirations or plans for the children were. Two-thirds of the Punjabis listed their own firms as the place for at least one of their children. More than two-thirds of that group, in turn, had one or more sons working with them. By contrast, only a little more than one-third of the Tamilnadu group aspired to have their children work with them; of that group, two-thirds already had one or more of their children in their enterprise. Twenty-five per cent of the Orissans thought sons should be in their business; about half of that proportion were, in fact, already there.

We also asked all respondents to rank a series of occupations in terms of "the respect you give them." Respondents in both Orissa and Tamilnadu gave almost half of their first place votes to "agriculturalist." Only in Punjab did "manufacturer" rank first, and by a

-substantial margin. It should be added that "agriculturalist" came in second in Punjab, with 15 first-place votes as compared to 27 for "manufacturer." In Tamilnadu, "teacher" came second, and "manufacturer" was third. In Orissa, there was no identifiable second category. Twenty-one Orissans ranked "agriculturalist" first. The remaining Orissan respondents divided about equally among all the other occupations except "moneylender."

In sum, then, commitment to industrial activity is weaker among the Tamilnadu group and Orissans than it is among Punjabis. We can understand part of this from an earlier context. Many of the industries in Madras, particularly those among the wealthier group, were established not to create new wealth, but to help protect the old. In Punjab, by contrast, small industry is more widely perceived as a vehicle to wealth. Even some of the Tamilian Brahmin small industrialists, who are not from commercial families, find themselves in industry from necessity rather than choice, having increasingly been squeezed out of other occupational categories through the imposition of quotas limiting their numbers.

The atmosphere of excitement surrounding industrial growth in Punjab conduces to an interest in manufacturing as a career. Construction for new industries radiates outward in almost all directions, one's relatives and friends are making money dramatically, and this visible activity generates its own momentum in much the same way that booms and panics take hold in the stock market. The rewards are clear and obtainable for many. If one has worked in a factory and learned a skill, then it is time to branch out on one's own.

In this regard, what is striking about Ludhiana, in particular, is just how common this attitude is. Most members of the labor force (often working side by side with owners and their families) are workers from the nearby state of Uttar Pradesh. Almost all manufacturers of other than knitted goods said that most of their labor was nonlocal, because as soon as any local person learned the business, he would set up on his own.

In one last way, Punjab is quite different from the other two states, and this is in association life. Formally, all the states have numerous voluntary industrial associations, such as industrial estate associations, hand-tool makers' associations, trunk and box-makers' associations, and so on. A substantial proportion of these organizations, however, are either honorific or a device by which a particular individual pursues his own end by establishing a paper association with himself as head. In Tamilnadu, for example, the president of the electroplating association used his position as an excuse to call on ministers of government, to explain to them the plight of electroplaters in general and his own problems in particular—not all of which always concerned electroplating.

What set some of the Punjab associations apart was their ability to work together to achieve functional ends. In Ludhiana, for example, the wool merchants' association had the task of allocating the limited available supplies of Australian wool among its members. Perhaps more interesting was the ability of Punjabi associations to function effectively as pressure groups. One example concerns the purchase of property in industrial estates. At the time when sheds in the estates were first rented, tenants in all of them were told that the government intended to sell the plots to their occupants at some future date. This became increasingly attractive to industrialists, because the fully developed land at the good industrial estates was clearly appreciating in value. Consequently, renters in estates in all three states tried to purchase their land. By 1975, only the Ludhiana people had succeeded. They claimed their success resulted from their superior organization, their development of extensive contacts in government circles, and their tenacity.

A second example was the 1972 lockout. During the period of raw materials shortages, states—like the factories in them—received allocations of materials to distribute. The size of the allocation was based in principle on the estimates of demand submitted to the central government by state officials. Punjabis were angry because they believed that their raw material quota was particularly inadequate. It is impossible to tell if this belief was true, but the manufacturers certainly felt it was. In each state, we asked respondents to tell us what their biggest problems were in conducting their businesses. The overwhelming response in Punjab in 1971 and 1972 was the problem of getting adequate raw materials. This was different from both Tamilnadu and Orissa, where respondents reported that a lack of finance was the overwhelming problem. We surmise that the rapid growth in Punjab's industry left Punjab with allocations inadequate to meet its rapidly expanding needs. Each state was clamoring for a share. Punjab, in the early days, had earned a reputation for demanding excessive quantities. Government procedures tend to be inflexible, and the rate of increase of raw materials production in India had come perilously close to zero.

Given that Punjab was the fastest growing state in small-industrial production, it seemed unreasonable that its manufacturers should suffer the most. The Ludhiana manufacturers, consequently, announced a lockout day when all the factories would be closed, and owners and workers would march in protest. We had watched other attempts at coordination and demonstration in India in the past, and had noted that they were usually disorganized and characterized by low participation. This occasion was different. Every factory in Ludhiana was indeed closed; we drove around to check and could not find a single exception. A large procession of trucks, cars, and buses proceeded in an orderly fashion to Chandigarh, the state capital, to demand more raw materials. They did not achieve their goal; there was really no way they could, but the feat itself was impressive. We doubt that anything like it could be achieved elsewhere in India, for it required a high level of organization and cooperation. It may be that the economic specialization and interdependence in Ludhiana, of which we have made much, created the solidarity essential to coordination.

In summary, the Punjabis created for themselves, or found themselves in, a situation that yielded large benefits from an extensive division of labor. The consequences of such a division were reduced entry costs and elaborate support facilities—from raw materials to marketing, good communication, heightened solidarity, an atmosphere that promoted optimism, and a great sense of possibilities—that encouraged reinvestment, even in times of temporary setback.

In Tamilnadu, by contrast, there was neither such a thoroughgoing division of labor nor the advantages that were inherent in such specialization. Where people made parts of things, they sold them to fewer, larger units, and they depended on contracts from big purchasers to succeed. A screw manufacturer in our sample, for example, reported that he was about to diversify his product because his three automatic screwmaking machines produced such volume that there were no big customers left to sell to, and he did not know what to do with the excess.

For the inverse reason, other small manufacturers had to make all the components of their product to be able to make the product itself. They were not able to acquire the range of parts they needed on the open market. By making relatively specialized whole products aiming at a specialized market, they too were able to survive.

Lower industrial densities do not generate the excitement that leads to a broadly positive attitude toward industrial activity. The more prosperous in our Tamilnadu sample were better educated than their Punjabi counterparts; they were more managerial and less participant in the activity of the industry. They preferred long-term secure contracts to open market activity; and they were less eager than the Punjabis to have their offspring work with them.

Lacking either the markets or the support facilities even of Tamilnadu, most of the Orissa small industries had the most difficult struggle to stay alive. Unless they made a consumer good that relied on local taste preferences and was fairly inexpensive per unit, they were required to establish enclaves with vast resources to succeed. In the state's preindustrial condition, many of the existing firms were almost a sideline. They lacked the networks and communication that characterized Punjab. Just as prosperity set in motion new opportunities for prosperity among the Punjabis, the poverty of Orissa was an almost insuperable obstacle to industrial development.

CHAPTER NINE

CORRUPTION

Lawbreaking is so pervasive in the Indian business world that it is difficult to discuss any aspect of industry without mentioning violations. At the same time, government policies óften invite, if not compel, such behavior. They have often been aimed either at making scarce goods scarcer, or requiring compliance with rules so complex and detailed that they encourage harassment by low-level, poorly-paid investigative officials who will be paid off to go away. Income tax evasion, black marketing, and bribery are all part of conducting business. As one respondent explained, "I must have broken more than a lakh (100,000) of laws in my work, for which I have paid out more than a lakh of rupees. Because I have a successful business, I represent an opportunity to be dunned at every turn."

It was with the problem of bribes that we began such a discussion in a previous publication (1969: 141). Let us set the stage here by drawing on it.

In America, we distinguish between tips and bribes. A tip is a legitimate token of appreciation for services rendered or services about to be rendered (e.g., the dollar slipped to the head waiter for procuring a table by the window). A bribe, on the other hand, is payment for "non-legitimate" services rendered. . . . Is the dollar to the waiter for the table by the window a tip or a bribe? To the extent that the money rewards the receiver, does not incur future obligations on his part toward the donor, and does not harm or potentially harm other people, we would (usually) say it is a tip. Otherwise it is bribe. Obviously, the distinction is not particularly clear in America. . . . [In India] it is a matter of different categories. One clue in this regard is that for many situations in which we would apply either the word tip or the word bribe, Indians use one word, *bakhsheesh*. As it is commonly used, bakhsheesh is simply money that changes hands, in many contexts. Money that one gives to a beggar is bakhsheesh (neither a tip nor a bribe to an American); money one gives to a taxicab driver in excess of the fare is bakhsheesh; and money one gives in many cases to keep the machinery oiled is, similarly, bakhsheesh. For many instances of what a Westerner might call bribery or corruption are, in the Indian context, simply bakhsheesh.

We then went on to distinguish between normative and non-normative bakhsheesh, as well as other normative and non-normative ways of stretching one's income. The small tips or bribes one pays to receive basic government services that are legally one's due are normative bakhsheesh. People come to accept their legitimacy if the demands do not become too large, and people share a view of what is too large. If one is a businessman, he accepts the necessity of making such payments as part of the cost of doing business, and figures them into his cost structure.

We met one young man in Tamilnadu and one in Punjab who, having been trained in the United States, objected strenuously to paying bakhsheesh for services they thought were legitimately theirs, such as a telephone installation or an inspection for a license. Each spent much time writing letters, fighting with officials, and trying to bring court cases while everybody around them thought they were utterly insane. Ultimately, the Punjabi's business failed and the Tamilian, becoming increasingly strident, was swallowed up in a series of complicated lawsuits.

Similarly, perquisites of office are turned to personal account, sometimes with wide acceptance, while other instances are seen as exceeding a widely-held norm. Two American examples of acceptable appropriation of perquisites are the office supplies American white-collar workers bring home from the office; and blue-collar workers' use of factory tools and equipment to make their own repairs—what Gouldner calls "government jobs." Each is an example of stealing; but each, if it does not become excessive—and most participants agree about what that means—is acceptable.

Another distinction, which crosscuts the normative-excessive dimension, is whether the corruption is productive, has no effect on production, or is detrimental to productivity. Each of these operates independently of whether or not it is normative. Let us illustrate by turning to one of the most pervasive areas of corrupt activity, the black market.

In 1971, almost every industrial raw material was scarce and subject to government price controls. Even materials that were not scarce could be used only under license and control by the central authority, because they had either been scarce recently or might be in the future. First among these was steel. Except for some specialized items, such as stainless steel and high carbon steel, which were imported, steel was manufactured in India. The wholesale price was determined at the mill head, and resale prices were also fixed. These prices were from one-half to one-third of what the same product would command on the open market. All other raw materials were treated similarly. Importation, distribution, and prices of nonferrous metals and wool, for example, were strictly regulated by the government. Food products such as molasses and sugar, and grains such as wheat and rice to be sold for milling, were also under control, as were coke and coal. Users of all these items were required to be licensed; users were expected to apply for allocations of scarce items at the controlled price based on their needs.

This discussion simplifies the process, of course. Different agencies handled different goods, and often followed different procedures. Since steel products were the most widely used, let us look at procedures and practices in that area as a model for all the other goods and processes. Steel prices were, as we have noted, determined at the mill head; volume users were expected to make their purchases and to arrange for them to be carted home. Many of these purchasers were not final users. They might, for example, be processors, such as rerollers who would produce desired shapes for industry. Since steel was scarce, such people were in a particularly good position to purchase at low mill prices and, subsequently, charge high prices for the work done on the product.

It was impossible for small-scale users to make their purchases at the mill, because they could not purchase at the volume required. Consequently, to make controlled-price raw materials available to small users, state agencies made the volume purchases, transported them to local stockyards, and then sold to small users at the controlled price. To get the goods, which were in very short supply, each small user was obliged to apply for an allocation from the state. The application had to be made some six months to a year before the anticipated delivery date, of course, to allow time for the paperwork involved in equitable distribution. After a user applied, an inspector would arrive on his premises to estimate his capacity, based on records of sales, size of factory, and installed machinery. On the basis of this investigation, a small factory would be awarded its allocation. (In these situations, small industrialists were in a cleft stick: they wanted to maximize capacity for inspectors and mini-mize it for tax collectors.)

The spread between the controlled price for steel, about Rs. 1,200 per ton, and the market price, about Rs. 2,200 per ton, was attractive. If one in fact manufactured a steel product, its selling price was based on the market price of raw materials rather than the con-trolled price. Hence, one could make enormous profits. Further, if one could receive an excess of controlled price raw materials, one could sell them at a profit without having to go through the process of manufacturing and selling the goods. Some individuals set up factories with no intent to make things at all, but simply to sell their raw materials. We observed several such nonbusinesses in each state. In these cases, one had the choice of trying to fool the inspec-tor, bribe the inspector, or try some combination of the two. Oppor-tunities for all kinds of larceny abounded. Some factories in Tamil-nadu were alleged to keep their machinery running with no workers at all, so that the electricity-use figures would square with what they said they were using in raw materials.

The techniques of exploiting the price spread were complex, and involved everyone who made anything from steel, from the most humble metal bender to the Government of India itself, which sometimes paid black market prices for steel to obtain material in time to complete an important project.

Metal benders might never see the sheets of metal for which they contracted. The moneylender who provided the money for the pur-chase picked up the sheets, sold them directly, and gave some proportion back to the metal bender. He, in turn, bought scrap metal or used steel drums to make his trunks, buckets and office furniture, both to sell and to provide the appearance that he was using his sheet allocation if he were inspected.

Such a system ramified widely. Suppliers sold black market steel but could produce bills reflecting a sale at the legal price. They customarily charged a 15 per cent premium for the extra service. Everyone kept two or three sets of books: one for the income tax people, one for the small industries department; and one that reflected the actual transactions of the firm.

Businessmen frequently resold goods or materials they had obtained through incentive programs at concessional prices. In 1971, imported machinery was available on attractive terms to small industrialists. All they had to do was to prove that they needed it. This machinery could be sold at a premium price to someone else when it was delivered. Loans were available to small industrialists at subsidized rates, provided that they were invested in fixed, not working, capital. Where people did not have to pay bribes that brought the cost of the loan up to the market rate—and our data show that this was often the case—loans were also lent again at the market price, or, on occasion, used to construct houses on the factory site rather than additional factory buildings.

Finally, exporters were entitled to import goods worth a fixed proportion of the total amount they had exported, provided that they could show that they used the imported materials to improve their export position. The exporter paid off the inspector who approved the purchase. He then sold the entitlement to others who collected the goods when they arrived. Some exporters sold their products abroad at | breakeven | prices simply to get the lucrative import entitlements. Some of them informed us that their income was more than twice what they reported.

Normatively speaking, the rules were quite clear and widely shared. Trading in steel and entitlements simply for the profit, though widely done, was not approved of; but everyone participated in the black market to balance inventories, and no one disapproved. If one had ordered rounds but received flats, he took them anyway and sold them so he could purchase rounds. If a minimum order was 50 tons and one needed 20 tons, he would take the whole order and sell the difference. If one expected his allocation to be delivered in two months, but he had a contract to complete in one month, he would buy the needed steel "in black" immediately and sell his allocation when it came. These activities were so widely practiced and accepted that the purchasing agent of an international corporation once insisted to us that they were legal.

All of these people were, to use the local language, bona fide users. At the next ethical level were the people who used only a tiny proportion of what they got, and who had created their firms with the intent to sell the raw materials. Their behavior, while unacceptable, was not heavily disapproved, because it was always possible that they might become bona fide users. We had at least one such person in our sample. He manufactured little tin boxes. He acknowledged that he entered the business because he had political contacts, and he intended to get illega' "heets and sell them. When his contacts were removed from office, he decided to use his machinery to make the product he was supposed to be selling. He was struggling to make a living doing that when we interviewed him.

Government officials in one of the states said that in the early days, allocations were given to people who were known to sell them off, because the government hoped that, once they had established a firm and gone through the motions of making a product, they would, in fact, start making the product. By 1975, one could test that proposition, for raw materials were no longer scarce. We saw little evidence to support it. These manufacturers were thought to be of dubious moral worth. Once, while looking for a manufacturer we had visited previously, who worked in a large yard with several other manufacturers, we had to ask where we could find him. "Oh, you mean 'Quota Jain'?" our guide responded. "Is he manufacturing anything these days?"

Those who did not intend to manufacture anything were viewed as still less reputable by all involved. Because shortages had become so intense, attitudes toward nonusers were malevolent. The greatest disapproval was directed at individuals who tried to corner the market for scarce raw materials so that they could charge more than the legitimate market price. Since these were very big businessmen, they were feared as well as hated, and placed along-side those who sold adulterated goods.

One nonuser class in Punjab, at least, did get modicum of respect. These were old men who had been in the knitting business, and who now, though more or less retired, still received their wool quotas. The difference between the quota price and the market price was about 40 per cent, so they sold theirs to proudce a little retirement income.

The normative situation changed over the years, at least in Punjab, where Pratap Singh Kairon, Punjab Chief Minister between 1955 and 1964, had told his officials not to be too zealous in checking on whether or not alleged users were bona fide users. He wanted to get as much raw material into Punjab as he could. The way to do this was to overrepresent demand when his officials met with central government officials to work out the allocation for each state. There is some consensus that is just what happened. Our searches for registered industries turned up more nonindustries in Punjab than in either Tamilnadu or Orissa, lending additional support to this belief.

In our judgment, most black-market activity, with the exception of the creation of artificial scarcity, is productive corruption. Underlying this view is the belief that market mechanisms are important for the allocation of scarce resources. Government policy aborted the workings of the market, creating, in so doing, a large class of middlemen who made money out of restoring the market function. The black market got goods to the people who really needed them: those who were either such efficient producers that they could be competitive even at inflated raw materials prices, or those whose products were in such demand that they could absorb the higher price in selling them. We should be clear here that we are referring only to the small-scale sector where, in our judgment, talk of market activity makes sense.

What's in the Black Box—An Aside

We continually wondered why, given rampant black-market activity and the vast spread between market and black-market prices, the government did not decide to charge the market price for steel at the mill and soak up the profit itself, instead of encouraging corruption, disrespect for law, and creating a class of middlemen who made the black market possible. Whenever we had the opportunity, we asked government officials connected to the raw materials policy process why this was so. We received three classes of answers, none of which really satisfied us. The first was, "But that would be dishonest. One should not take advantage of an unfortunate situation to make extra money. The shortages, after all, are partly our fault." Price should be pegged to cost; better yet, to what the cost "should be" and not to "what the market would bear." This particular informant shared a widespread conception of market prices. To charge what people are willing to pay is exploitation. When we pointed out that this policy had generated an extensive black market, the response was "Yes, we must be tougher in enforcement. But businessmen are such bloodsuckers." The government officials' hostility toward business seemed to combine elements of socialism with elements of the traditional economic system, which held businessmen in low esteem.

The second response was a more cynical one. The middlemen who make the money, some said, were the people who supported Mrs. Gandhi and the Congress Party. Such policies were deliberately encouraged so these men would prosper. In this case, we tried to find evidence from our informants that this was so, but were unable to do so. The third response was that the pricing policy was an inducement for someone besides government to take the responsibility for distribution. With excellent profits to be made, goods were moved optimally. Since the government was already spending enormous sums on its own allocation system, which the black market in effect negated, this was not a satisfactory answer either. We concluded that the first response was probably closest to the truth. The belief that price should be related to cost of production, not in itself unreasonable, was widely held. The history of businessmen cornering the market and charging what it would bear had made individuals deeply skeptical of the market process. Further, it was inescapable that if one wanted to encourage the growth of small industries, efforts had to be made to see that small producers would get the goods at the same price the big purchasers paid. No matter that, in the end, small purchasers paid higher black-market prices. If enforcement of the law could have been improved and if subordinates had not been so corrupt, small businessmen would in fact have gotten goods at the lower price.

Indian officials often doggedly pursue control and supervision even if that pursuit is both impossible and self defeating in the face of other goals. The State Trading Corporation's activities were the only exception to this orientation that we came across in the 1971 period. The STC was at that time managed by Prakash Tandon, the former Chairman of Hindustan Lever, who often saw the virtue in charging market prices for some materials under STC control. He did not, however, go all the way, distinguishing between goods for the privileged and goods for everyone else. Where goods for the privileged were concerned, he reported, he was predisposed to "sop up" whatever profit he could. At that time, STC was buying used imported automobiles from their foreign owners at the prices the cars would have commanded in their countries of origin and then auctioning them to the highest bidder at prices often five times as high. Since these imported cars were clearly aimed only at the luxury market, the practice was in line with the general principles Tandon avowed.

Other Productive Corruption

Corruption flourished around the enforcement of the Factory Act and other legislation designed to improve working conditions. The Factory Acts in India specify the number of days and hours a worker may work, the number of workers one may have before being obliged to contribute to pension funds, the ages of workers, the number of cubic feet of air space each worker must have, a standard for lighting, the number of toilets per worker, appropriate clothing, and a host of other requirements.

These regulations are relatively more enforced in Tamilnadu than they are in Punjab. We saw very few young boys working in the Madras factories we visited. By contrast, their presence was almost commonplace in Punjab. Punjab factories looked less safe than their Tamilnadu equivalents. In Punjab, wires hung dangerously and machines were so crowded together that it was hard to imagine how workers could work at them. One Punjabi staple cloth manufacturer had so many looms filling his living room that the only way to get across it was to crawl.

The government's attitude toward enforcement, too, varied by state. We interviewed state small-scale industries directors to ask about their activities. Only in Madras did the director volunteer, as his first item of information, that his job was to enforce factory laws. In Orissa and in Tamilnadu, many more respondents complained about being harassed by inspectors than did the Punjabis, who hardly ever saw one. The Tamilnadu respondents told of endless difficulties, too, in getting licenses, and listed the numerous licenses they were required to have. Whatever the formal licensing requirements may have been in Punjab, by contrast, our Punjabi respondents often had difficulty remembering any at all.

Close supervision and control have several negative consequences for productivity. Complying with manifold rules and regulations raises entry costs in industry. The average size of initial industry investment in our Punjab sample was Rs. 21,000; the average size in Tamilnadu was Rs. 99,000. This may be one reason, along with the advantages of the greater division of labor, why Punjab has so many more small industries than does Tamilnadu. One can start up an industry in the living room, put one's wife and children to work, and gradually expand. The only requirement that must be met in Punjab is to get a "no objection" certificate from the neighbors. Since all were doing the same thing, no one could reasonably object. In Tamilnadu, by contrast, we found a small unit that had been closed because the neighbors objected.

Enforcement of factory legislation can become a legitimate vehicle for harassment and petty corruption. Because so much activity is controlled and circumscribed, businessmen must in principle fill out many forms and comply with numerous procedures. This is so time-consuming that many larger industries keep a full-time liaison officer in New Delhi to deal with government procedures. A small-scale industrialist manages his own business, markets his product himself, recruits employees, buys raw materials, and the like. Other pressures on his time mean taking time from productive work to deal with them. The Indian government was aware of this problem, and officials talked at the time of the research about having a single, all-purpose inspection rather than the numerous inspections then required by different agencies. By 1975, nothing had come of it.

As things stood then, the busy industrialist had to deal with inspectors from the Health Department, and with three or four representatives from different units in the Industries Department, the Electricity Department, the Excise Tax Department and the Inland Revenue (income tax) Department. If he had a violation, or a violation was alleged against him, he might need to close his business for a day or more to go to the office and deal with the authorities. The easiest way out of all this was simply to pay off the numerous inspectors; hence, the quotation at the beginning of this chapter about the man who had violated 100,000 laws. As Punjab illustrates, by comparison with Orissa and Tamilnadu, the corruption involved in looking the other way instead of enforcing manifold confining regulations has the consequence of increasing productivity.

Normative Nonproductive Corruption

Four sales-related practices that occurred in all three states had the consequence of producing windfalls at one time and setbacks later. These practices are: giving kickbacks in the private sector, giving kickbacks in the public sector, using political pull in the public sector, and seeking seals of approval.

Kickbacks in the private sector seemed to be most institutionalized in Tamilnadu. Because small-scale producers depended on orders from a few giant manufacturers, access to those units' purchasing agents was crucial. Purchasing agents received somewhere between 10 and 20 per cent of the value of the purchase in exchange for agreeing to buy a particular producer's goods. During our stay in Madras, a company purchasing agent was caught doing this by management. Apparently, he had been demanding ever higher kickbacks, and was becoming increasingly high-handed about it. Would-be suppliers complained; an investigation revealed that the purchasing agent had gotten too cocky. He was living in a house that no one at his salary could afford; he owned two cars although a motor scooter would have been more appropriate; in general, he had an excessively high standard of living. He was fired, and the contracts of virtually all the small suppliers who were beholden to him were terminated. In our own sample, we came across two factories with investments of several hundred thousand rupees that had to be sold, because without those contracts owners could not maintain them. Both factories were reduced to small machine shops making fabrications to order.

Winning public sector orders also required kickbacks. Government officials and bidders colluded on large contracts. For smaller orders, for which bidding was unnecessary, suppliers made payments. There seemed to be agreement that payments of 5 to 10 per cent of the total sale were reasonable. Some people in Orissa allegedly demanded 15 per cent. This was considered greedy.

Having a friend, relative or ally in government who would look out for one's interests—directing orders, quota allocations, and not-very-carefully-investigated subsidized loans—was a special case of the kickback system. In India, even more so than in the United States, the government is the largest employer and purchaser. Additionally, quasi-government agencies such as the Madras Port Trust supplement government-related opportunities. One's sales could soar or collapse depending on which way those resources and orders went.

The fourth case is a little more complicated. Government agencies sometimes made loans for equipment, providing a list of approved manufacturers of products, such as diesel engines, that might be bought with those loans. If one manufactured such a product, one had two goals: get on the government's approved list, and keep as many others off that list as possible. One would then have high rates of sale. In Punjab, one manufacturer we met actually went into business producing diesel engines because he was guaranteed that his product would be on a short list. Starting from nothing, this company's sales rose to Rs. 3.5 million in two years. Small local companies competed with large national corporations as well. We met a salesman from a national corporation who explained that his major task as a salesman was to visit government officials in each state and persuade them to place his company's product on the approved list.

In the diesel engine case, the bubble burst. Farmers, who used them to power irrigation pumps, complained that many diesel engines on the market were much cheaper than the authorized product (Rs. 1,500 as compared to Rs. 2,500). The approved list was subsequently abolished. The bottom dropped out of the manufacturer's business (which was coincident with a general decline in the demand for diesel engines as electrification was replacing diesels in rural areas); luckily, he had extensive resources that enabled him to hang on for two years, until he found a new successful product.

All of this activity was normatively acceptable. The government's efforts to authorize suppliers for recipients of government loans also seem, in the abstract, to be somehow reasonable. Low income farmers may not be knowledgeable enough to evaluate new kinds of machinery and the government's attempts and to protect them seem a responsible approach. In practice, however, things did not work out that way.

The windfall profits of a few manufacturers probably do not have much effect on productive capacity where capacity itself is great. The rise and fall of a few manufacturers in such a setting makes little difference in the overall picture. Certainly this was true in Punjab. Where capacity is less, as in Tamilnadu, the desire for a guaranteed profit (and the real possibility that one might achieve it through such a deal) may have discouraged people without guarantees from entering business.

In Orissa, manufacturers looked for politicians who would deliver windfalls to them, but politicians also looked about for up-and-coming manufacturers to whom they could funnel funds. They would take a cut of these funds and, as they became more wealthy, would provide economic support to the politician. The problem was that the few businesses that were succeeding in this difficult environment were highly visible to politicians on the prowl. They found each other and properly cared for each other, and the businesses grew apace. Any skills a growing industrialist might have developed—to make a good product, to deliver the goods on time, to market properly—became largely irrelevant. The consequence was that when the politician lost power, the business would plummet, perhaps never to recover. A modestly successful business, employing people, selling goods, and making some contribution to the economy, might evaporate without a trace.

In Orissa, we were struck by the disproportionate success of a few Muslim-owned firms. When we asked the owners about contact with government officials, they all reported virtually none at all. During the 1960s, Orissa experienced disruptive anti-Muslim riots. Almost all of our Muslim respondents lost something during that period, and found government officials notably unsympathetic when they sought compensation. They had a real fear of getting tangled up with the official world, and did everything possible to keep their distance. We hypothesize that the very desire to stay away from government officials may have benefited their business activity. They prospered by succeeding at what they did rather than by colluding with politicians or turning government incentives to their advantage.

In all three states, people hid their incomes. Large black-market income from dealing in raw materials and imported goods was one reason. Another was the steeply progressive income tax. Concealing income was normative behavior. Mrs. Gandhi's efforts at reform during the 1975 state of emergency included tracing unaccounted-for money. The homes of the wealthy were raided by police, and records were examined in detail. The main thrust was a "turn in your ill-gotten gains" program. Businessmen were told that if they reported all of their unaccounted-for money, they would be forgiven any previous penalties (although they would be required to pay back taxes on those funds—which at then-prevailing rates would typically amount to most of the money). People who did not take advantage of this opportunity, it was announced, would be dealt with mercilessly, stripped of their wealth and thrown into jail (the right of habeas corpus having been suspended). Officials of the Inland Revenue Department traveled to businessmen's clubs and associations, carrying that message with them.

We talked to one industrialist who had just come from such a meeting. The Inland Revenue official had really talked tough, saying "I know all your names. And I know what you have been up to. Turn in your unaccounted-for money or you will get it." We said, "And as one man, you all marched up to the podium and turned your pockets inside out?" "Oh, no!" he responded. "We are made of sterner stuff than that." Although normative, this kind of corruption did discourage production. Hidden money was converted into jewels and gold rather than productive investment.

In sum, widespread corruption is in part the consequence of the government's desire to control closely many aspects of economic life in an effort to foster equity. This effort, however, results in illegal activity, much of which is necessary if private sector industrialists are to remain in business. In Punjab, the lax enforcement of formal restrictions had the positive consequence of encouraging entrepreneurial activity. High-ranking government officials there understood that lax enforcement had positive results in achieving the state's long-term economic goals.

To understand corruption, we have distinguished between normative and nonnormative corruption and among corruption that has positive, neutral, or negative consequences for production. Later, we discuss different meanings of rationality to explore further just how far government policy, derived on rational grounds in the service of some goals, ultimately had the consequence of being non'rational, both because it was unenforceable and because it conflicted with other goals among which no system of priorities had been established.

CHAPTER TEN

MODERNIZATION AND INDUSTRIAL GROWTH

Ambiguity about the relationship between modernity as a psychological construct and industrial growth as a process characterizes virtually all of the literature on modernization since the end of World War II. Implicit in the literature is the idea that modern men are necessary to economic growth, but the relationship is seldom specified in detail. Where industrial growth is related to modernization, industrialization is often the independent variable; Inkeles, for example, shows how factory work helps to develop modern attitudes among workers (1974: 154ff).

Although it may seem self-evident, we want to begin this discussion by asserting that industrialization is the core process of modernization. Any list of modern countries includes all the industrial countries of the world; the less modern are also the less industrialized. Any rank-ordered list of modernized countries would correlate highly with a list based on steel consumption per capita (see, e.g., Marsh, 1967).

One way to understand the process of modernization is to look at the behavior of industrialists—those responsible for growth—in capitalist countries as a way to understand the process of industrialization. Notwithstanding their key role in growth, the label "modern" is not necessarily one that can comfortably be applied to this group. In fact, using measures similar to those others have used, we will show that there is nothing systematically or identifiably modern about our Indian industrializers as a group. We will also discuss how attitudes commonly believed to be prerequisites for modernization may have little to do with whether people *behave* in ways that help to effect economic growth. People may hold traditional values and even behave in certain traditional ways while behaving in modern ways on those dimensions crucial to success.

This chapter looks briefly at key pieces in the literature to high-light these points. We then turn to our small-scale industrialists to see if their profiles can help us understand why scholarly expectations about modern attitudes may not be very useful.

Although the literature on modernization has ich and varied antecedents, its post-World War II contributions begin with Daniel Lerner's *The Passing of Traditional Society* (1958) and extends through Inkeles and Smith's *Becoming Modern* (1974). Lerner begins *The Passing of Traditional Society* with the parable of "The Grocer and the Chief." Both men live in a poor out-of-the-way village in Turkey. The 63-year-old chief is contented with his life. "What could be asked more? God has brought me to this mature age without much pain, has given me sons and daughters, has put me at the head of my village, and has given me strength of brain and body at this age. Thanks be to him."The grocer, by contrast, when asked whether he is contented, says, "I have told you I want better things. I would have liked to have a bigger grocery shop in the city, have a nice house there, dress in nice civilian clothes (p.23)."

When asked what he could do if he were president of Turkey, the chief answers, "I am hardly able to manage a village, how shall I manage Turkey?" The grocer, asked the same question, responded, "I would make roads for the villagers to come to towns to see the world and would not let them stay in their holes all their life. (p.24)."

And when each was asked where he would live if he had to leave. Turkey, the chief responded, "Nowhere. I was born here, grew old here, and hope God will permit me to die here. I wouldn't move a foot from here." And the grocer replied, "America, because I have heard that it is a nice country, and with possibilities to be rich even for the simplest persons (p. 25)."

In Lerner's view, the chief is traditional; the grocer is a moder-nizer. Underlying the difference is the fact that the merchant has "empathy," or "the capacity to see oneself in the other fellow's situation (p.50)." Included in this is the ability to want new things and to begin to imagine how to get them.

The growth of mass media, urbanization, and education all assist in this process, promoting flexibility and openness to new expe-riences, and infusing a "rationalist and positivist spirit."

To Lerner, as people become more flexible, imaginative, and empathic, a modern society will appear. Industrialization has little part in this picture. That the increased wealth industrialization will bring might hasten modernization is not recognized. What is needed, according to Lerner, is to generate more empathic men who can imagine new things and want them, and to create a political system that allows them to achieve change in a measured fashion.

Inkeles and Smith attempt to make Lerner's analysis more systematic and to add dimensions other than empathy to modernity but they still avoid the question of how those who score high on a modernization scale are going to develop their country, except in the tautological sense that the level of a country's modernity is proportional to the fraction of its citizens achieving high scores on a modernity scale.

While believing that "modernity" is necessary to achieving industrialization, Inkeles and Smith do not ask how having more modern men helps to increase industrial production: "(W)e doubt that (a nation's) economy can be highly productive, or its political and administrative institutions very effective, unless the people who work in the economy and staff the institutions have attained some degree of modernity (p. 9)", and "We feel our results make it clear that as developing nations acquire more modern institutions, more widely diffused, to that degree their populations will come to include more and more men marked by the characteristics we have termed modern (p. 298)." The implicit notion here is that a "modern" society both requires and generates modern people.

Through developing the modernization scale, the scientist, according to Inkeles and Smith, can learn things "we need to know in order to make intelligent choices among programs for effecting social change (p. 278)," that is, how best to induce modernization.

The Inkeles-Smith definition of modernity is a compendium of numerous desirable attitudes set against another list of undesirable attitudes labeled "traditional."

From a desperate clinging to fixed ways of doing things, some of them moved toward readiness for change. In place of fear of strangers and hostility to those very different from themselves, some have acquired more trust and tolerance of human diversity. From rigidity and closed-mindedness, they have moved toward flexibility and cognitive openness. They now seek to break out of passivity, fatalism, and the subordination of self to an immutable and inscrutable higher order, in order to become more active and effective, and to take charge of their individual lives and the collective destiny. . . . Some ethnic and religious groups also seem more likely to generate individuals of this type. Swiss

Protestants, East European Jews, Parsis in India and the Ibo in Nigeria all seem to qualify (pp.4–5).

This list of communities does not strike us as being characterized by flexibility and cognitive openness. This is certainly the first occasion on which we have heard of Swiss Protestants and East European Jews being singled out for their trust and tolerance, never mind flexibility and openness. All of the groups mentioned, it is true, have been successful entrepreneurs in the changing worlds in which they found themselves; but entrepreneurship is not what Inkeles' and Smith's book is about. The Ibo may come closer than the Swiss Protestants and the Eastern European Jews. They are probably also less entrepreneurial, succeeding best in government service and the professions. The Parsis lie somewhere between the extremes represented by the other groups.

The confusion here is typical of the literature. Eager to make the highest values of Western society equivalent to modernization, one reads backwards and makes entrepreneurs look as if they fit into that general framework. Nonetheless, the nature of that crucial relationship between modern outlooks and industrialization is not made explicit.

Part of Inkeles' analysis derives from the functionalist perspective mainly attributable to Talcott Parsons, but also characteristic of the work of Germani (1968: 343ff) and Levy (1966). People who follow this approach often find a particularly good fit between cultural traits and the structure of the society in which they are found. The analysis of "fit," however too often slides into one of "necessity," as if those characteristics found in a society are required for the existence of that type of society. Yet, it seems to us curious to assume that because a particular set of cultural attitudes has been observed to occur in societies that are also highly industrialized, that pattern is therefore *required* before industrialization can be expected to occur. To observe a concurrence is not to demonstrate that no other combination of characteristics is possible. Moreover, the observed state of affairs may have arisen after the nation has become industrialized, and be quite different from requirements conducive to the process of industrialization itself.

Two central components in most discussions of modernization are kinship and religion. Let us begin our analysis with kinship, for "no institution of society is more often depicted as either an obstacle or a victim of modernization than the extended kinship structure" (Inkeles and Smith, 1974: 25). We will move from discussion of the family structure to consideration of women's and children's roles as well as efforts to limit family size. Because they are so obviously related to each other, we shall consider the role of the extended kinship structure in the family firm.

Family Structure

One reason that the nuclear family household has been seen as necessary to an industrialized society is empirical: seventeenth-century England, where the industrial revolution began, had nuclear family households. But there are other sources for the argument that extended kinship structures are inimical to development. The old Parsonian evolutionary perspective assumed that the more differentiated social systems are, the more efficient they are, and argued that just as whole societies evolve toward more differentiated forms, so the evolution of family structure follows the same process. Indeed, it is the quintessential process that illustrates the larger theoretical form. The Parsonian argument emphasized the potential lack of fit between family goals and business goals and the possibility that, where family and firm overlap, business goals may be subverted by family needs. This argument also points out differences in value orientation between families and modern business enterprises. The family is affective, has more than mere functional concerns for its members, is ascriptive by definition (people are born into it rather than achieving membership in it), and is particularistic—that is, it treats members in particular ways by virtue of their membership. Modern businesses, by contrast, value people for what they can do rather than what they are. They are universalistic in recruitment, affectively neutral in interpersonal relationships, and functionally specific in focusing on organizational goal achievement. In the Parsonian view, conflict between the two styles is inevitable where the two structures are intertwined (Parsons, 1961; White, 1961).

Related to that argument is the idea that organizational authority structures will be defined by the familial authority structure of the society in which it finds itself. In a patrilineal extended-family system, the father—or, in the absence of the father, the eldest brother— is the head. Managers must be recruited among family members, restricting the choice of people available to take on important roles. One can argue, as Parsons (1961) did, that this kind of household, in which an elder still holds sway, is less willing to innovate and is more predisposed to do things in the traditional fashion than is the isolated nuclear family. A more general non-Parsonian economic argument (although still a functional one) is that extended family life limits geographical mobility for the labor force. Too many members have to be moved at any given time for movement to be feasible. Such a restriction acts as a drag on the system.

To investigate this question, we asked respondents who besides themselves lived in their house with them. Excluding 18 ambiguous cases, our sample divided almost equally into nuclear and extended family households, 86 of the former and 88 of the latter. Comparing family type with level of success, using as the measure of success either gross revenue or our own assessments of business success (failing, holding its own, profitable), we found no relationship between family type and business success, either for the sample as a whole, or for Tamilnadu or Punjab individually. Orissa is an exception, and an exception, as Table 1 illustrates, that runs in the opposite direction from what would be predicted by the theory.

Table 1
Success of Enterprise, by Family Type: Orissa

	Failing	Holding Own	Profitable	Total
Nuclear	4	5	5	14
Extended	0	15	9	24
Total	4	20	14	38

Chi Square = 8.07 $p < .02$
Gamma = .30

Among the extended families, there are no failures and a disproportionate number holding their own. Although the numbers are so small that we are reluctant to make too much of the differences, examination of the table does suggest one reason why Orissa may be different from the other states. It is the only one in which the largest category for all small industries is "holding its own." Our guess is that the line between failing and barely succeeding is thin; the industries in the latter category are also at the low end of the economic spectrum. In Orissa, the opportunity structure is so restricted that family businesses will persist as long as an enterprise provides them any living at all. In other states, businesses at the same level would be labeled failures. In both Punjab and Tamilnadu, there is less incentive to stick together, because more occupational opportunities are available. Industries just holding their own are not attractive enough; sons will leave the family and seek other occupational opportunities.

Why doesn't the relationship between family structure and business success hold? We propose two hypotheses: one we cannot test at all; the other, we can explore impressionistically. The first posits that what appears to be a nuclear family at a given point in time may actually be an extended family at a particular point in its life-cycle. That is, longitudinally, an extended family exists until a father dies; after that, sons usually divide, each again to create his own extended family which will stay together until that founder dies. This might explain why nuclear families are unsuccessful in business: they are not "psychologically" nuclear families but only de facto nuclear. This is not, however, an explanation for why extended families succeed. To understand this, one must look at how an extended family household operates. Joint family businesses have succeeded at one time or another around the world, and the successes of the small industries we studied suggest that things in the joint family household may not be what they seem, especially from the perspective of an American theoretician.

To begin with, we believe that the patriarchal structure of Indian families—in which elders are responsible for career decisions of their offspring and, to a lesser extent, of their younger siblings —conduces to a more unsentimental and rational (universalistic and achievement-oriented) orientation toward offspring than one finds in a typical American nuclear family. Americans in India are often struck by the almost coolly calculating judgments Indian parents make about their children's abilities, and the instrumental way in which they apply those judgments. "This one is good at math; he will go into engineering. This one is not so smart; we will send him out to do some job." This orientation extends to the allocation of duties and obligations in the family business. Children are trained according to their perceived capacities and are given assignments appropriately. This may mean, incidentally, that a child, or a son with his wife, will be sent away from the family to study, to work, or to open a branch of the family business. Belonging to an extended family does not necessarily mean that one is forever locked into the physical domain of that family. This orientation is not particularly Indian, and it may be true wherever extended family businesses succeed. Stephen Birmingham, for example, reports that in the nineteenth century, when one of the scions of a big German Jewish banking family was sent off to open a branch in the new city of San

Francisco, the patriarchal father sent along a younger brother as well. The elder was thought likely to be a dreamer, and the down-to-earth younger sibling was expected to remind him that there was work to be done.

Similarly, just as modern organizations have informal lines of authority that do not coincide with formal authority structures, so extended families have working authority structures that do not mirror the patriarchal hierarchy. Although the patrimonial and authoritarian structure of the Indian family remains intact, fathers and sons are able to discriminate between social authority, where the formal structure is maintained, and business authority, where it is applied flexibly.

Fathers told us on occasion that they were unhappy with some of the business decisions their sons had made, but that times had changed and so had levels of technological skill. Many fathers in our sample reported that where technological expertise plays an increasingly important role, where government programs and laws shift rapidly and require close attention, where markets and the structure of the economy are changing, their sons knew more than they did. This was not simply talk. It was observable in the interplay between father and son in our interviews, and in the allocation of responsibility and decisionmaking.

The balance of authority in such relationships is a subtle matter. Fathers were consulted about all business matters, whether or not it was appropriate. Indeed, discussion of business was an almost continuous family matter among the men. In one family, where three generations worked together and the fourth was getting ready to enter the family business, the old grandfather was almost deaf and very feeble, but he was included in the conversation and his views solicited. At the same time, it was absolutely clear that on business matters the initiative was with his sons. By contrast, fathers (and grandfathers) were still very much in authority on social matters, although the children's views were relevant. This old man, for example, was permitting the education of his female grandchildren, although it was clear that he did so with misgivings.

There are other examples. Maninder Singh had been a landlord in what is now Pakistan. After Partition, he was given land in India as compensation for his losses. The land was of much poorer quality than the property he had left behind. Accustomed to being a large landowner, it looked as if he was doomed to live in genteel poverty. At his son's urging, however, he sold his property and invested in a foundry. As the foundry prospered, his son suggested that they go into the manufacture of small parts, using a brand name, which would guarantee reliability. This would give them an advantage they did not enjoy in their business of casting parts to order in the foundry. A good quality manufactured product, he argued, would generate its own demand. That was, in fact, what happened. Demand was so great that they had to allocate their output among their customers.

Although they operated a relatively modern business, the Maninder Singh household was still a traditional one. They were strict vegetarians and the men and women did not mingle. Maninder Singh decided when and whom his sons should marry, and he chose uneducated wives for them. He himself went on annual religious pilgrimages, and the family made substantial contributions to the Golden Temple at Amritsar. In the house, the sons did what their father asked, be it running a small errand or subjecting their own children to various religious ceremonies.

The difference between social and business authority was illustrated during one of our interviews. Our respondent had organized two small firms with family capital, over the misgivings of his father, a third generation trader in grains and oilseeds. Father and son displayed in their dress and manners the startling life-style disjunctions between generations that are common in India. The father wore traditional dress, sat on a slightly raised portion of the floor near the door of the warehouse, had little formal education, and knew no English. His son wore a shirt and pants, sat at a desk, was a college graduate, and spoke English. When the younger Mr. Agarwal ordered Cokes for us, his father called out in Hindi, "Don't give him that; give him a real drink." Without hesitation or discussion, the son signalled that the Cokes be removed and proposed to the interviewer that he drink chilled, flavored milk fresh from the family buffalo instead. The ensuing discussion between father and son presents a further problem for theorists of modernization, who see traditional men as lacking empathy. The son in this case appeared to be more modern than the father. He explained to his father that he had ordered Cokes because Americans drink them often. Father's response was, "Anybody who comes all this way in such hot weather wants to learn how *we* do things. He can drink Coca-Cola in America."

The evidence shows, then, that the family authority structure is not necessarily replicated in the business structure. This holds true for brothers as well as fathers. We were surprised at the number of younger brothers who actually ran family concerns while their older brothers were allotted responsibilities of a lower order. We do not mean to suggest by this that the authoritarian nature of the family structure is relaxing or changing. It is relaxed—for all we know, it always may have been—in a functionally specific context. One of our interview questions posed this dichotomy: Is it more important for a 12-year-old boy to obey his elders or learn to think for himself? Only 44 respondents selected the "think for himself" option. Some respondents explained that we were confusing India and the United States: there was no way that a 12-year-old Indian boy could learn to think for himself even if that was all right for American children. The answers to this item did not show any relationship to business success, nor did we expect them to, although prolonged dependence of chidren is clearly part of the Indian cultural pattern.

A second problem extended family enterprises are thought to face is the problem of recruitment of quality personnel. One is limited, so the argument goes, to family members, who may not be the best candidates for the managerial positions available. In extreme cases— where, for example, a family has no children or has only daughters—this argument may have some force. Even here, however, matters are not so simple. One family business in our sample was run very effectively by a daughter. Other sonless fathers may select sons-in-law and bring them into their businesses. Two such cases are in our sample. Childless couples in India often adopt nephews who will become their heirs. Three of these were in our sample.

More important, however, is to understand the implicit point of comparison: that is, the open recruitment of managers. Obviously, for most small-scale firms, recruiting top quality managers is not possible. Yet, family businesses have advantages that are often overlooked. Family members are assets as both managers and laborers: they work long hours, and the overlap between work setting and home allows members to think about business and discuss it all the time. The younger family members grow up knowing the business. While still young, they accumulate the experience of working and of listening to the men talk about business decisions. In short, loyalty, hard work, and intimate knowledge of the business are advantages in recruiting family labor. Extended families are able to mobilize more capital than isolated nuclear households. The joint family household is cheaper to maintain, particularly under Indian conditions, than its components would be if the family were dispersed. Paying for only one house, making one-time investments in shared consumer goods such as clothing, refrigerators, radios, vehicles, and the like, and sharing of housework among the women, bring living costs down. Our evidence supports the idea that extended families can mobilize more capital for investment in an enterprise than nuclear families can (see Table 2).

Table 2
Initial Investment in Industry, by Family Type

	Low	High	Total
Nuclear	51	31	82
Extended	45	52	97
Total	96	83	179

Chi Square = 3.9 $p < .05$
Gamma = .31

To summarize, family structure is apparently unrelated to business success in the small-scale sector in India. Many of the difficulties alleged to affect the small family business are mitigated by mechanisms within the family structure itself, and other aspects of the overlap between family and firm may have beneficial consequences for the enterprise, at least in the small-scale sector.

Several questions about the long-range prospects of family enterprises remain. First, will the successful among them be able to navigate the transition, as the industry grows and moves from exclusive family control to reliance on outside professionals for provision of some of the needed managerial skills? Some in each state did so during the period of our study. In addition, most of the large industries in India are built around families—the Tatas, the DCM (Shri Ram) Group, the T.V.S. group in Tamilnadu—who have been professionalizing their firms by hiring trained managers.

Second, can a successful family enterprise maintain continuity through several generations? We were struck by how much thought our respondents gave to that question. The more prosperous ones did often establish independent units for the sons, facilitating a split should a death or an acrimonious dispute require it.

Finally, the question whether the small-scale industry will be an important form in the long term for contributing to India's industrial production was still unanswered in the 1970s. At that time, small-scale industries constituted an important sector on the industrial scene, steadily increasing output while the balance of industrial activity was lethargic. The small-scale sector has continued its dramatic growth into the 1980s. Prime Minister Rajiv Gandhi, moreover, has expressed interest in encouraging this sector. This suggests that small-scale industry will be more than a transient phenomenon.

We find the evidence compelling that at a minimum, the family business is a valuable transitional agent, making a substantial contribution to economic growth, not in spite of being a traditional form of organization but because of it. Its advantages in mobilizing resources, both human and material, its ability to command the respect of the society in which it is embedded, and its flexibility in the face of changing conditions combine to make it a peculiarly effective agent for incorporating change and providing important social cement at the same time.

Let us turn now to two other aspects of family life alleged to go with modernity: family planning and the liberalization of women's household role (Inkeles and Smith, Portes). In the modernization literature, family size correlates inversely with modernity (Inkeles and Smith, p. 108; Portes, p. 24). The urban and the educated, it is alleged, for whom children are more obviously an economic liability than they are for rural populations (for whom, it has been argued, more children provide more agricultural hands) restrict family size. Generally speaking, industrialized countries produce fewer children than do non-industrialized ones; and the better educated produce fewer children than do the less well educated.

Our own data do not fit this model, nor did we expect them to. Our respondents viewed additional offspring either as more labor or more management, depending on the size of their enterprise; sometimes they waited to expand their businesses until the children were old enough to play a significant role. For some of them, at least, rational behaviour included augmenting family size rather than restricting it.

Amont the families in our sample, the average number of children was 4.3, the mode being 5. We computed a family-planning measure by counting the average number of children people had per year during the first ten years of mariage, excluding those with no children as infertile. (This procedure was suggested by Donald Bogue). We then ran this measure against business success, measured both by gross income and our own assessment of profitability. We could discover no relationship. We introduced controls by age, because we thought it possible that young families might be more likely to practice birth control, and young families just starting out might look less successful, but the younger people in our sample were often in successful family businesses, so that possible effect was reduced.

Because one could argue that those in extended families might more likely be conservative because of the influence of elders, we checked to see if family structure was related to number of offspring; but the practice of family limitation showed no relationship to the structure of the family or to business success.

The Position of Women

An argument in the modernization literature is that opening opportunities in society leads to freeing women from their traditional subservient role. Inkeles and Smith found a correlation of .50 between concern for women's rights and their modernization scale. We have two ways to measure attitudes toward women. First, we asked respondents:

a) Some peopole say that educating one's daughters beyond reading, writing, and arithmetic is a waste of money.
b) Some people say that nowadays girls must have more education than formerly, but sons must still be given the most because they must make their way in the world.
c) Some people say that nowadays it is just as necessary for a daughter to have education as it is for a son.
   Which of these views do you think is correct?

Naturally, there is slippage between expressed attitudes and real behavior. One of our most Western-seeming respondents insisted that girls should be as well educated as boys. Nonetheless, he had not educated his daughter beyond matriculation (high school), but was planning to send his son to college. (He himself was a college graduate.) When we pointed out the discrepancy to him, he answered, "yes, but my daughter's husband-to-be does not want an educated wife."

We found no relationship between business success and attitudes toward education of daughters. When we look at the distribution of those attitudes in each of our states, we find that 65 per cent of the Tamilnadu respondents believed daughters should be as well educated as sons, as compared to only 53 per cent in each of the other two states; however fewer Punjabis thought that daughters should have no education at all. The Tamilnadu respondents, then, express slightly more modern attitudes than the others. When we compared these findings with measures closer to behavior, the picture looks somewhat different. We asked respondents whose children had completed their education how much education their children had had; we asked those whose children were still in school how much education they expected their children to have. We then constructed an index from a ratio comparing higher education of sons with higher education of daughters. An index of 1 signifies that the education levels are equal, numbers greater than 1 indicate more education for males than females, and numbers less than 1 indicate the reverse. On this measure, Tamilnadu and Orissa suddenly appear very similar, with indices of 2.3 and 2.2, respectively. Punjab has an index of 1.1.

Without making too much of this, it nonetheless confirms an impression we have already reported in another context: the Tamilnadu group appears to be more Western (or "modern") than the Punjabis partly because they are better educated and have a distinctively English kind of public style. That appearance, however, does not cut very deeply. Just as the Tamilnadu entrepreneurs often seemed not quite to be entrepreneurs, their expressed attitudes about women were incongruent with their behavior toward them. The Punjabis, by contrast, were less well educated and not particularly westernized in style, but had a smaller disjunction between expressed attitudes and behavior. The Orissans were the most consistent.

In summary, then, we can say that family structure, family size limitation, and attitudes toward the education of women had no connection to industrial success. Extended families had advantages for some during the industrialization process; and large family size is at least as rational a choice as family size restriction for small-scale industrialists. Finally, attitudes toward women were unrelated to industrial success.

Religion and other Variables

Because of Max Weber's concern with the relationship of religion to the rise of capitalism, and his exploration of those ideas in his study of India, Indian religion has been widely thought to inhibit economic growth (Kapp, 1963; Rose, 1970). Weber argued that Indians lacked a set of beliefs analogous to Protestantism that would both demystify the world and drive people to reinvest. At the same time, Indian beliefs, such as the fatalistic cycle of rebirths, the caste system, and a preoccupation with magic and other mystical components of the Hindu religion were obstacles to economic growth.

Hinduism is characterized by a dread of the magical evil of innovation. Even today the Indian jute peasant can hardly be moved to fertilize the land because it is against custom. In addition to this, Hinduism places its supreme premium upon caste loyalty. The salvation doctrine of Hinduism promises rebirth as a king, noble, etc., according to present caste rank to the artisan who in his work abides by prescribed traditions, never demands overpay, never deceives as to quality. In the often cited principle of classical teaching: "it is better to fulfill one's [caste] duty even without reward than someone else's no matter how excellently, for therein always lies danger. The neglect of one's caste duties out of high pretensions unfailingly is disadvantageous in the present or future life" (Weber, 1958: 122).

It is dangerous to take religious texts at face value as sources of conduct and guides to action. Western Europeans and Americans know that it is easier for a camel to get through the eye of a needle than it is for a rich man to get into Heaven. Nonetheless, many pursue wealth avidly. By contrast, Indians regularly pray to the goddess Laxmi to bring them wealth; and businessmen and students pray with great passion to the god Ganesh to help them overcome obstacles. To watch these rituals, one would assume that Hinduism emphasizes pursuing wealth and surmounting obstacles in the quest for self-improvement. Hindu religious texts were produced by one group, the Brahmins, that had a vested interest in maintaining a ritual and social order structured in their favor. To assert that ancient Brahminic prescriptions for behavior are a valid statement of actual, contemporary behavior is, of course, fallacious.

Weber learned what he knew about India from reading religious texts and secondary sources. Even an empirically-oriented social scientist, particularly if he is a Westerner, may have difficulty understanding the role of religion in Indian life, both because our own orientation to religion is so different, and because Indians often express themselves in terms that one might think confirmed Western analyses of them. Several respondents told us they were performing their "traditional" occupations when in fact they were in occupations their fathers had newly entered ten or twenty years before. People say it is their duty to do something when they mean that it is what they want to do. Milk purveyors water the milk; it then becomes their caste duty to water the milk. Part of the problem is in the translation of the word *dharma*. Usually translated as *duty* as in Weber's discussion, a more sensitive rendering might be *nature,* as in "the nature of the beast." "It is the nature of milk sellers to water the milk" certainly moves the sentence closer to the idea here. In fact, the practice is no different from the American practice of filling ricotta cheese with gelatin, gum, and chemicals and calling it ricotta cheese, or reducing the amount of product in the box and calling it "new and improved." Businessmen the world over use tactics of this sort, but in India, someone will explain that they do it because it is their tradition or their duty.

Work, we were often told, is sacred. Even without a Protestant ethic, many of our successful respondents worked long hours and had little leisure time, much like their American counterparts who are featured in *Fortune* magazine. Their work environment was especially constraining: materials shortages, difficulties in raising cash, labyrinthine government regulations, and electrical power cuts and failure were all part of a normal working day.

The prevalence of ritual and the willingness of Indians to explain their behavior in traditional terms may mislead an observer. One respondent described the elaborate ritual activities he was obliged, as a good Hindu, to follow daily. We asked him when he found time for it all. "Of course we don't really *do* all these things," he explained. "If we did, we would not have time for business." On another occasion, we were driving with friends down Mount Road (now Anna Salai), the Fifth Avenue of Madras. Our hosts were quite orthodox Hindus, they said, and probably were. One of them was intensely involved in studying the Upanishads, and both were wearing sacred markings on their foreheads, having recently come from prayer. The conversation as we drove down the street was: "See that building over there? Ramaswamy got it for a song. I understand he has worked out an unusual rental deal with Lufthansa." "Who owns that building?" "Ramanathan. I hear they had had a terrible time with construction costs; they were unable to get the steel they needed, and had to use a heavier and more costly grade." The conversation was the sort that real estate investors carry on the world over. Detailed knowledge of who owns each parcel and what he is doing with it is essential to success. People in similar occupational positions, albeit in different societies, often behave similarly regardless of cultural differences. The structrue of external constraints pushes them toward the behavior necessary for them to succeed.

Small industrialists in India sign contracts to produce goods by a particular time, at a particular price, and of a particular quality. If they fail to perform, they may forfeit a bond. They may not get subsequent contracts. If their prices are too high, they will not get contracts. If their prices are too low, they will not make money. To get the working capital they need, they must establish relations with creditors and a reputation for paying back their debts. We belabor these points only because scholars have insisted with straight faces that secularism is essential to industrialization, and the practice of religion is an obstacle to rational behavior (Germani, 1968: 344, 348; see also Levy, 1966. 606–18).

Successful manufacturers must, in certain essential respects, behave similarly, regardless of the society to which they belong. There will be differences, too. Rules about bribery and attitudes toward law enforcement, for example, may be different, and in that sense, different environments may require different behaviors; but the basic structure of the situation, imposed by the need to operate efficiently and profitably, is unambiguous, and imposes unambiguous constraints on the parties involved. At the time of our visit, an old friend who was a first-generation industrialist from a wealthy landowning family had trouble meeting a contract on time and had to refinance a loan, both to be able to fulfil the order and to keep from going bankrupt. "How can you allow yourself to get so much in debt?" his thoroughly appalled, upright family wanted to know. "If I did not allow myself to get into that situation, I could never make any money," he correctly replied.

Weber claimed that Hinduism creates a fear of innovation. Many of our respondents continually innovated, in the modest way that manufacturers usually do. They bragged about the new machinery they designed. One respondent won a prize in an international competition for his incubator design. He subsequently experimented with nutrition supplements for animal feeds. Others were proud that they were the first in India to manufacture their product. Still others asked us about the latest designs from America. Bicycle parts manufacturers in Punjab wanted to know about ten-speed bicycles. An eyeglass manufacturer in Tamilnadu who had been manufacturing bifocals was eager to handle contact lenses. A cookie manufacturer wanted American recipes. The best of them acted like hustling businessmen anywhere, quite independently of their attitudes toward religion.

Weber was right in asserting that Indian religion is mystical and magical. Indian life is pervaded with spirits, with belief in astrology, with the belief that ancient mythical tales are an accurate historical account—just as some people in the United States believe in the literal truth of the Bible. We have already reported on the modern young man whose family kept elephants. They also maintained a small temple, complete with busts of the family god and of Mohandas Gandhi. The temple was built around an ancient tree, among whose roots lived a cobra for whom they put a bowl of milk out nightly, scrupulously following religious prescription. Yet the young man was no less effective a businessman.

Often when we began to talk about astrology and religion during our interviews, someone would produce a man who was an expert at reading palms. Sophisticated people would huddle together over our palms, commenting and evaluating. Several offered to have our horoscopes cast by their family astrologers, but we were unable to produce the exact time of our births, necessary for the horoscope to be completely accurate. Respondents talked about ghosts who walked in their factories at night. Religion, the mystical and magical, surrounds one; it does not intrude on the conduct of business in ways that influence outcomes.

To confront this question more systematically, we included five items tapping commitment to traditional aspects of religion in our questionnaire. We asked respondents how religious they thought they were compared to others; whether they thought astrology was a science that predicts human behavior; whether, as some had asserted, the ancient books *Ramayana* and *Mahabharata* indeed had examples of airplanes, television sets, and cannons; and about the relationship of hard work to God's will in determining successful outcomes.

Setting our criteria for a significant relationship at p less than or equal to .05 and gamma of .2 or better, we found no relationship between attitudes and business success. These findings may seem surprising. Many of the attitudes expressed have apparent real-world implications. About half of the respondents thought that astrology was a science that could predict outcomes. Yet, belief in astrology did not have any consequence for business success. Similarly, a belief that airplanes, cannons, television sets, and the like were described in the ancient *Ramayana* and *Mahabharata* seems to reflect an unscientific mentality, but it has no consequence for business success.

We think there are two reasons for this. First, whatever their belief systems, industrialists function in the real world. The feedback they get there is far more important to their business decisionmaking process than are their spiritual beliefs. Second, people segregate their religious beliefs from the world of work (Singer, 1974). When we asked respondents if a belief in astrology was a problem for them in conducting their business, they often looked at us incredulously. They did not use astrology for making business decisions or, if they did, it was just one piece of pertinent information among many. After all, if astrologers could accurately predict the outcomes of different business decisions, they would all be rich themselves. Astrologers were seen as particularly valuable in deciding on children's spouses, when to take a vacation, how to get on better with one's in-laws, and the like. There are, then, both appropriate and inappropriate spheres of action for astrological investigation.

Those more familiar with Western ways compared astrologers to psychoanalysts. "You go to the astrologer as a psychologist. He pats you on the back; he explains that things are bad now because the stars and planets are such and such a way. But things will work out. When you come to see him for an interview, you come back with a real sense of relief, an intense sense of relief. I have the habit of visiting our astrologer when things are not going well, and he helps." But the respondent did not stop there. "But also, my astrologer—and I say this as an engineer and a scientist with a little embarrassment—my astrologer has made predictions and they have all been correct. I am not saying that that is because astrology is a science. I don't believe that, because my training won't allow it. But he has not yet been wrong. Our marriage based on horoscopes has worked out very well, and we are very compatible. She is also a graduate and we are a mentally compatible pair. But beyond that, he has made a set of predictions, and they all have come true. I don't believe in it. I can't give you any satisfactory explanation." This man manufactures sophisticated electronic equipment, which he sells to multinational corporations.

The respondent who manufactured the prize-winning incubator for chicks, and is now marketing feed supplements for livestock, reported, "It is a science. But I myself do not go to astrologers at all. Because I don't want to know my future. I prefer to live on that wonderful human idea called hope."

In his famous essay, "Magic, Science and Religion," Malinowski notes that the vitally important practice of canoe building in the Trobriand Islands is intensely involved with magic. People know that magic does not help them to build strong canoes. People with technical skills do that work. Nonetheless, magic has an important role to play.

> We find magic wherever the elements of change and accident, and the emotional play between hope and fear, have a wide and extensive range. We do not find magic wherever the pursuit is certain, reliable, and well under the control of rational methods and technological processes. . . . Magic suuplies . . man with a firm belief in his power of succeeding; it provides him also with a definite mental and pragmatic technique wherever his ordinary means fail him. It thus enables man to carry out with confidence his most vital tasks, and to maintain his poise and his mental integrity under circumstances which, without the help of magic, would demoralize him by despair and anxiety. . . . (Malinowski, 1954: 19).

In Indian business, one uses ritual to deal with the uncontrollable or to explain and justify bad luck. As the electronics manufacturer said, it helps to take the pressure off. One is soothed so that he can get back into the fray, where he uses the utmost rational means to achieve his business goals.

Another informant, a businessman who had not been a small-scale industrialist, reported how that process worked for him. His joint-family business had broken up with acrimony on all sides. There had been illness in his nuclear family, followed by a death at the same time as the blowup with his father and one of his brothers. "I was in the blackest despair. What had I done that such evil should befall me? I went to my family astrologer, who explained that I was suffering a temporary setback because the planets were in an unpromising conjunction, which would last about six months or a year. Knowing that, I did not feel so badly, and I set back to work."

With another brother, he opened a new distributorship in the fastest growing town in the state, and began to emphasize service as well as sales; he also set up a small-scale fabricating unit with a few machines on the grounds so that he could get black market raw materials and sell them.

We seen, then, that much of what seems to be magic performs the function Malinowski attributes to it. Rather than discouraging rationality in contact with the real world, it helps people deal psychologically with the uncontrollable.

Almost all discussions of Hinduism lead to caste, an attribute of Hinduism so distinctive that it often receives disproportionate attention as an explanatory device in accounting for differences between Indians and those from other societies and cultures. There now exists a body of literature demonstrating that the caste system is not the obstacle to industrialization and change that it superficially might seem to be (see Morris, 1965; Singer and Cohn, 1968; Lambert, 1963). For our purposes, it is useful to think of castes as endogamous, locality-based social groupings identifiable by name. While "castes" as used in Hindu texts number only four, arranged in order eternally and immutably on the basis of their ritual purity, castes in the real world number in the thousands. These are variably assimilated to the four castes, or *varnas,* of the Hindu texts, and are accorded by others a ranking of ritual purity that may or may not be unambiguous. These groups are often, though by no means always, associated with a particular occupation.

Small-scale industry in India is not restricted to a narrow group of castes. Eighty-five caste names appeared in our sample. Variability is even greater than that nomenclature appears it one refers to endogamous groups, since even within a locality, for example, some Brahmin groups do not intermarry with others (Aiyars and Ayengars in Tamilnadu, for example); and because castes with approximately the same name in different regions do not intermarry. That figure excludes, too, 5 of 34 Sikhs (who, although technically without caste, often maintain caste names and self-identification), 4 Jains, and 9 Muslims.

Ten per cent of the respondents were Brahmins, and 3 per cent were untouchables. Caste names associated with agriculture (Mudaliar in Madras, Kandait in Orissa, and Jat in Punjab), writing (Karan, Kayastha), and a host of other activities all appeared. Of course, there is no traditional industrial caste. There are, however, castes associated with trade (Chettiar, Sahu, and Aggarwal), which is often antecedent to industrial activity. There are regional groupings which, following Indian usage, we shall call communities (Gujaratis, Marwaris, and Jains). They constitute approximately one-third of our respondents. A final category comprises castes or communities with artisan names (Ramgarhia or Viswa Karma) that may also be protoindustrial.

The small-scale sector is hospitable to a wide range of caste backgrounds. When we look at who is willing to do business with whom, we find that people do business across caste lines. We informally asked respondents from whom they bought and to whom they sold, and in our observation of business transactions, caste was not a restriction.

This is not to suggest that caste is completely irrelevant to the conduct of business. Members of the same caste or community often had ties to each other, reinforced by blood relationships and intermarriage. These relationships facilitated communication and business dealings in general. Networks based on particularistic ties made it easier for some to enter certain businesses than others, and for them to get word of good opportunities in advance of others. In this sense, these groups are similar to some ethnic occupational groups in the United States. Several writers (Glazer and Moynihan, 1963; Lieberson, 1963) have pointed out that when a particular group dominates an industry—Jews in clothing manufacture and retail trade, Greeks in the restaurant business, Italians in construction, Chinese in restaurants and laundries—members help each other succeed through shared information, job contacts, and contracts. In Ludhiana, bicycle parts manufacture is heavily dominated by Ramgarhia Sikhs (although there were very successful non-Ramgarhias and even non-Sikhs) and sewing machine assembly and sales by Aroras. In Madras, textile manufacturing is dominated by Chettiars. Growing up in a family where business is always discussed and having relatives in the same or related industries facilitates entry and success. Nonetheless, about one-third of our respondents are not from artisan or commercial castes or communities, nor are their fathers in occupations connected with industry, such as tradesmen, businessmen, manufacturers, craftsmen, shopkeepers, industrial personnel, or artisans. That third is about as likely to be doing well as the others. No doubt, fewer people coming from nonbusiness-related backgrounds choose small-scale industries as a career; however, when they enter the field, they appear to do about as well as those with previous connections.

These observations are confirmed indirectly by the only macrodata we have seen on mobility rates in India. Shupe and Hazelrigg (unpublished) analyzed mobility rates for a national sample of Indians, ignoring caste, to determine how Indian mobility rates compared with those of other countries at similar stages of economic development. They found Indian rates were just what one would have predicted based on its economic status alone. That is, the caste system, for all of its alleged rigidity, seems irrelevant for understanding mobility rates. Like religion, caste is relevant for some spheres of behavior, but not for others. It is as important as ever for choosing marriage partners, and for numerous ritual activities. Just as Americans function well together across race in the workplace but do not socialize much at home, caste is not particularly relevant for making business decisions. Its sphere is ritual activity and, to a somewhat lesser extent, social interaction.

We have now dealt with a series of variables commonly considered significant to a tradition-modernity scale. Family structure, attitudes toward family planning, and the socialization of young men are all supposed to be relevant to something called modernity (Portes, 1973). Although in our data some of these variables are related to each other, they are not related at all to industrial success. Similarly, intensity of religious belief, particularly as it applies to Hinduism, and commitment to the more magical and mystical aspects of religion, are thought to be important. Again, none of the items shows any relationship to business success.

Adherence to the culturally-prescribed family pattern, a long history of not educating daughters, not practicing family planning, and following the tenets of an ancient religion exemplify what most scholars would call "traditional" behaviors. Indians we know make the same distinctions, although they might call them old-fashioned or old-style, as in, "they have a real old-style household. You know, joint family, puja (prayer) in the morning, and so on."

Writers in the Lerner and Inkeles and Smith tradition, however, want to include something else that might be called psychological predispositions. Included here are empathy, awareness that others hold other views, openess to new experiences, efficacy, planning, a sense that what happens in the world is calculable, and aspirations for a better life.

We do not know what to do with these dispositions because we believe that most people in most places share them, although their differential access to information may influence how they respond to questions designed to measure these qualities. Further, to put them in categories called "modern" and "traditional" is to rob them of meaning. In any industrialized—"modern"—society, individuals vary in the extent to which they are empathic, flexible, and efficacious. In fact, when we look more closely at the items that are not related to family or religion, we realize we have seen them before; only instead of being called traditional and modern, they were called authoritarian and nonauthoritarian (Adorno et al., 1950), stereopathic and nonstereopathic (Stern, Stein and Bloom, 1956), and—for mental hospital personnel—custodial and therapeutic (Gilbert and Levinson, 1956). We are back in the epithet tradition of social psychology, where the good guys are seen as open, flexible, able to take the role of others, and willing to take rules with a grain of salt; and the bad guys ("High F" for Fascist, stereopathic, and custodial) are rigid, orderly, rulebound, non-empathic and ehnocentric (the last now appears in Inkeles and Smith as having "parochial allegiance"). We could divide any population, no matter where it stands on the scale of industrialization, into the white hats and the black hats, and discover, as both the old-style name callers and the new have discovered, that level of education accounts for most off the variance.

In our judgment, skilful industrialists are calculating, aspire to a better life, are open to innovation in business matters although not necessarily in social ones, value education, have a sense of efficacy, and admire technical skill. They have to be that way to succeed. But they are not more or less modern, for these attitudes are independent|of the characteristics discussed above. They can at the same|time be narrow, parochial, and hidebound in a range of non-business areas, and many of our respondents are.

This does not take away from Inkeles and Smith's more general point. In fact, it supports it. Although selective processes work to determine who becomes a small-scale industrialist, there is little doubt that those who succeed probably become better at what they do by the experience of doing it.

Business Plans

As Alex Gerschenkrohn has written,

> [I]ndustry requires fixed capital. . . . It demands construction of buildings and acquisition of machinery whose contribution to output must be utilized over a considerable period of time. This means that an industrial entrepreneur must look far ahead into the future (1968: 129).

Operating a small industry requires planning, so we asked respondents to tell us about their future business plans, and then categorized respondents by the degree of specificity of those plans. We classified "expand my business" or "improve my business" as vague. A plan to purchase a particular new machine or to begin producing a particular new product, or any other plan that included discussion of detail, we coded as specific. Unlike family size, family structure, aspirations for education, and all the religious variables, reporting specific plans correlates highly with business success by all of our measures of business success. Tables 3 through 5 show the relationship for all respondents, using reported gross revenue, our assessment of profitability, and the difference between original and current investment as measures of success.

Table 3
Profitability, by Business Plans

	Failing	Holding Own	Profitable	Total
Vague	8	25	21	54
Specific	4	24	59	87
Total	12	49	80	141

Chi Square = 12.4 $p < .001$
Gamma = .51

Table 4
Reported Gross Revenue, by Business Plans
(in Thousands)

	Up to Rs. 50	Rs. 50 – Rs. 250	Over Rs. 250	Total
Vague	34	15	9	58
Specific	22	26	43	91
Total	56	41	52	149

Chi Square = 21.5 $p < .001$
Gamma = .59

Table 5
Difference Between Original and Current Investment,
by Business Plans
(in Thousands)

	De-crease	No Change	Up to Rs. 50	Rs. 50– Rs. 250	Over Rs. 250	Total
Vague	2	26	12	6	5	51
Specific	1	26	17	18	23	85
Total	3	52	29	24	28	136

Chi Square = 11.0 $p < .03$
Gamma = .43

Education plays a role in the propensity to plan. Among the well-educated, so many did plan specifically that the relationship between planning and success weakens. Among the uneducated, however, it is strengthened. Education can teach people to be analytic about their work (see Tables 6 and 7).

Table 6

Difference Between Original and Current Investment, by Business Plans, High School Education or Less
(in Thousands)

	De- crease	No Change	Up to Rs. 50	Rs. 50– Rs. 300	Over Rs. 300	Total
Vague	1	22	7	5	3	38
Specific	0	13	10	10	13	46
Total	1	35	17	15	16	84

Chi Square = 11.2 $p < .03$
Gamma = .53

Table 7

Difference Between Original and Current Investment, by Business Plans, Education Beyond High School
(in Thousands)

	De- crease	No Change	Up to Rs. 50	Rs. 50– Rs. 300	Over Rs. 300	Total
Vague	1	4	5	1	2	13
Specific	1	13	7	8	10	39
Total	2	17	12	9	12	52

Chi Square = 3.8 $p < .43$
Gamma = .22

Our data show that the more people plan in a concrete and orderly way, the more likely they are to achieve business success. This is not surprising. What is surprising is to call good business-men "modern" and bad ones "traditional."

Most of the variance attributable to almost all the modernization items in the literature comes from education; the next largest comes from urbanization. That is true for many of our sites as well. We think that much of this research is measuring informational content that can be imparted either through formal education or through being close to information nodes—cities, factories, and markets—where information is widely diffused.

Although variably educated, urban respondents often surprised us by the information they had at their command, particularly as it pertained to the conduct of their business. As we reported earlier, even the least-educated sheet metal workers had detailed knowledge of how the black market worked. Even the Orissan horn carver entered national competitions for his type of product, and knew the virtues of having an illustrated catalogue that he might be able to send abroad. Our industrialists knew what they needed to know to conduct their business; and often, they wanted to know more.

Our analysis leads us to reject the sort of functional attempts that relate different kinds of belief systems and structures to one another. Similar belief systems and similar structures can perform different functions in different settings. People change more quickly and easily than the literature on modernity and tradition would have one believe. This is especially true if they can learn the consequences of their behavior quickly and if the costs of trying new things are calculable and not excessive.

Very little of the literature on modernization relates directly to the process of industrialization. The entrepreneurial route, it is true, is not the only one to industrialization. Successful industrialization, when executed by the state, may require a greater number of compliant workers and fewer entrepreneurs. Where industrialization takes place through entrepreneurship, however, industrializers quickly learn how to change their behavior to increase the likelihood that they will succeed. Those aspects of their lives that can meaningfully be called traditional can be segregated or reinterpreted to help improve their work situation. As in the case of both family structure and reproductive habits, the modes of behavior customarily called traditional serve quite well to help them achieve their aspirations. Religion, with its accompanying magical and mystical forms, is also used in instrumental ways where necessary, and serves other purposes where it does not interfere. In this view, people change their behavior when they need to for success; they change their beliefs much less, and they do not change their beliefs at all if the beliefs do not interfere with the achievement of other goals.

Finally, it does make sense to try to determine what makes for successful industrialists as compared to less successful ones if one is trying to understand the process of industrialization. In our own

analysis of values and attitudes, clearly the practice of careful analytic planning separates the successes from the failures. But this
approach to industrial activity operates independently of belief systems and general attitudes, and can even be independent of
education.

This is not to suggest that values play no role in the process of
industrialization and economic development. We have a strong
feeling that values help to explain differences among rates of
growth in our three states, but those values do not enter into the
process at the individual level in the way that our theorists of
modernization suggest. Instead, they help to provide an atmosphere, a context which hinders or facilitates the process. Independent of the obvious differences in resources among the states, institutional orientations toward the independent industrial process may
be hostile or at least not facilitating. The man in Tamilnadu who
told us that his in-laws did not prize his activities and the government official who saw enforcement of factory laws as his main
responsibility were reporting on constellations of beliefs that create
a climate in which it is difficult for individuals to function as free-
wheeling entrepreneurs. By contrast, the atmosphere in Punjab
clearly supported entrepreneurial activity at all levels. A pervasive
question in modern sociology continues to be how to link micro-
level behavior patterns to macrolevel outcomes. The atmosphere
that conditions entrepreneurial activity in each of these states may
be one way in which they are linked.

CHAPTER ELEVEN

THE PROGRAM:
IMPLEMENTATION AND EFFECTS

Although the small-scale industries program was well conceived, its impact on the growth of industries was difficult to measure. Small-scale industries grew in number and output through the mid-1970s, but the role government activity may have played in the process is not clear. One problem is to define criteria by which to judge the program's success. If success means encouraging founding new firms, then the program's role was small. In the sample, only 3 firms received loans from the government at their inception; one of those also received advice, as did one other. If success is measured by increased new investment, the program also had scant impact. Many of the small-scale firms founded after the program began were established by people who had extensive investments elsewhere; they hoped that a small industry would insulate them from onerous and threatening pressures from the government itself. If success means encouraging the little man, the program was hardly successful. Virtually all of its assistance went to big men. Indeed, the very structure of the program, despite the rhetoric to the contrary, with its security requirements and the volume of forms and papers to be dealt with, meant that the little man did not have the resources to take advantage of the offered incentives.

Part of the problem was that the officials' fears that the program's resources would be misused actually encouraged misuse of those resources. The government's obvious mistrust of industry made businessmen suspicious of the government's motives in offering incentives. The government gave with one hand and took away with the other. Additionally, it is easiest to encourage change through incentives where people are predisposed to accept change

and already have the capacity to use the incentives. Orissa exempli-
fied this. Trying to induce industrialization by incentives, facilitators, and exhortations there was like trying to push a thin rope from
behind. It will writhe, but it will not move forward.

In India, policy making is more rationalistic than pragmatic. In
June 1966, the Indian government devalued the rupee, hoping that
devaluation would reduce the international prices of Indian goods,
boost export sales, and improve the balance of trade. Government
officials were aware, however, that some products had sold well on
world markets at the higher predevaluation prices. Reducing the
prices on those items would result only in lost revenue. Some
officials saw an opportunity for the government to profit from this
situation. By charging export tariffs on these goods, their world
prices would be unchanged, and the difference—the tariff
receipts—would go to the government.

So far, all this appears reasonable—or, at least, rational. If, however, world prices of certain goods, such as minerals, fluctuate,
sometimes very rapidly, then problems will arise. One of the products to which the export tariff was applied was manganese. Manganese producers argued that since prices for their product were
volatile, the government duty would harm them by reducing their
flexibility in worldwide negotiations. Government officials
thought the manganese manufacturers were simply greedy (as one
would expect businessmen to be), hoping to make excessive profits. After all, they were doing quite well at the existing world price.
Officials decided the solution was to monitor world prices and
adjust the export duty on manganese accordingly. Again, this
sounds rational; but, except in crisis situations, the Indian
government rarely acts quickly. World manganese prices fell, but
the Government of India did not reduce its export tax. There was a
price below which Indian manganese traders would not sell. Sales
plummeted.

The lesson Indian government officials learned from this experience (replicated with other commodities as well) was, "we must
learn to react faster." This still sounds rational. Learning to react
faster is the rational solution only to those of a decidedly non-
empirical temperament, however, since the government could not
learn to act quickly. Given India's need to earn foreign currency,
the truly rational solution was the pragmatic one: abolish the
export duty.

Some American political scientists distinguish between ideological politics, which they fear, and interest politics, which they do

not (Feuer, 1969; Bell, 1960). Ideological politics are not governed by real-world constraints; because people believe the ideology forms a consistent whole, they make a great effort to make everything fit together. Because that consistency seldom occurs in nature, ideological politics tend to become increasingly coercive and, in the sense that we mean it, nonpragmatic. Interest politics, by contrast, do not require that all parts fit together in a seamless web. Instead, they pursue explicit, tangible goals that—unlike ideological solutions—are negotiable.

Ideological solutions are, unfortunately, the ones the Government of India often chooses. It decides in principle how problems should be solved, without allowing for the difficulties inherent in implementation. In a frictionless world, such an approach might make sense. In the Indian world—in any real world—where interests vary, communication is not easy, acts are hedged by efforts to avoid responsibility for outcomes, and following procedures faithfully would overburden everyone, it is unworkable. A government caught between its beliefs and the real world may appear recalcitrant and coercive to its constituents. Because of the rigidity of its formal structure, its constituents perceive it to be intractable. Bribery appears to be the best route for circumventing it. This dynamic informs much of Indian administration.

India's small-scale industrialists operate in a hostile environment. The societal commitment in principle to socialism combines with the conventional belief that those who make money (the village moneylender is the archetype) embody evil leads many administrators to believe businessmen are out to cheat them and the public (Taub, 1969). Many in India believe that, given the opportunity, businessmen will denude the country of foreign exchange by underinvoicing goods (having the extra money sent to foreign bank accounts), cheat consumers through adulterating and misrepresenting products, exploit labor, and pocket inordinate profits. This view is neither all right not all wrong. Given the government's rationalistic, interventionist orientation, however, the resultant controls themselves encourage immobility and corruption.

The second ingredient in the Indian rationalistic approach to policy is an abstract commitment to equity: a fair distribution of goods and services up and down the social ladder and across the country's many regions. This commitment is a natural response of a democratically elected, socialistically oriented government in a poor country. Commitments to equity are certainly desirable, but there are different routes to achieve that goal. Where distributable resources are limited, indirect means of achieving equity may have surer payoffs. Allocating resources only to those endeavors most likely to succeed might produce more benefits, which could be shared by all, than merely distributing resources equally to all, regardless of their ability to use the resources productively.

Two examples illustrate how such choices are made, and how, given a more pragmatic orientation, they might be made more effectively. As we discussed in Chapter Two, Orissa's primary industrial estate is in Cuttack. In 1975, its occupancy rate was 50 per cent. Industrial estates in Orissa's rural areas had even lower occupancy rates. Yet, in 1971, state officials had been pressing for more sheds in rural areas. Clearly, that kind of effort was a waste of resources. By contrast, every piece of subsidized industrial land in the Ludhiana area has been taken up. A new Focal Point industrial area had sold the first two hundred plots it had prepared in 1975, and 1,600 additional applicants were waiting. The Punjab government, which is in fact more pragmatic than those of Orissa and Tamilnadu, had written off its idle rural industrial estates and was trying to find other uses for the buildings. An even more pragmatic solution to the problem of encouraging industry might be to make more land available around Ludhiana and subsidize it less. Instead, an artificial scarcity had been created, bringing with it new opportunities for taking *bakhsheesh*. Even here, the rationalizing mind was at work. The government had fixed prices for all plots. Applicants were required to submit a plan describing the item to be manufactured, the kinds of machinery to be installed, and the total output anticipated. Electricity requirements had to be estimated. Preferences were given to people who would start new industries rather than expand old ones, and to people who were willing to install their own generators. Committees would be required to decide which products were the most needed, and to evaluate the quality of the plans and the design of the production process. Given the pressure from industrialists who wanted that space, it is clear that these procedures could never be realized.

The raw materials black market also illustrates the lack of official pragmatism. Committed both to the promotion of small industries and to equity, the government devised a system of allocation to permit small manufacturers to compete with large ones. The logic of the problem required that small industrialists get cheap raw materials; but providing cheap materials created the fear that people would take advantage of the situation. The next step, therefore, was to create controls—forms to fill out, inspections to undergo—to prevent cheating. The procedures were so complex, however, that their effect was the opposite of what was intended. The smaller small-scale industrialists had neither the time nor the skills to follow the procedures. Moneylenders could do it for them, however, and sell the goods on the black market. People who did not produce any goods also had the time. Prosperous manufacturers, who did not need to buy their goods so cheaply, could afford a functionary to carry out the necessary procedures. All of this does not even consider the question of the need to pay *bakhsheesh*. Except for a few devoted producers and people at the bottom of the scale, then, everyone in the system was able to make something for himself out of the process.

None of this is uniquely Indian. In the United States, developers used federal government money, intended to help house the poor, to build middle-class housing. The Federal Housing Authority programs aimed at helping the black working class have been mired in scandals, as have various Small Business Administration programs. The difference is that the Indian programs are more far reaching and comprehensive than their American equivalents. In the case of steel, the pragmatic solution, as we suggested earlier, would have been for the Indian government to charge market prices. Then no one would get price preferences; there would be no opportunity to make money by reselling materials, and no transactions requiring a black market. The solution chosen by the government was to fight the black market with increased vigor. Caught in the web of the system, as the state governments are, the pragmatic solution was the Punjabi one. Do not inspect, do not check, get as much steel into the system as one possibly can.

The program most highly touted by the government during the late 1960s was a subsidized lending program for small industrialists. Rates ran from 4 per cent to 7 per cent as against 14 per cent in the market. Ironically, it probably would have been adequate in that period simply to make loans, even at market rate, because banks were not giving small-scale industrialists loans at all. The loan program was so attractive that the officials responsible for administering it became extremely anxious. Evaluating applicants was a stressful process at best. The more an applicant needed the money, the more likely it was that his social class, ethnic, and educational backgrounds were quite different from those of the officer charged with evaluating his loanworthiness.. One concern, of course, was the possibility of default, which would make the official who had given the loan to the defaulter look bad. There is some evidence that in America, white loan officers deal with their insecurity about how to evaluate black applicants by simply denying them loans. In Orissa, officials merely established evaluation procedures that made it almost impossible for applicants to get the money. The Orissa Director of Small-Scale Industries—the only official we interviewed who tried to conceal details of the program's implementation because it looked so bad—told us about his selection process.

> To begin with, I make him come back to me a number of times, each time giving him some job to do, just to test his sincerity and persistence. Then also I check out his project with great care, and also find out about his personal qualities. The loaner must know the loanee very well. You see, we expect him to live frugally in the beginning—he should ride a bicycle, and not expect to drive a car right away. His habits are very important, because we have a stake in him. We need to know if he drinks, because if he does, we do not want to help him—he cannot afford to drink.

Under these circumstances, it is easy to see why no loans had been made by that officer. Indeed, in some years, the state had been unable to disburse all of its loan funds. Nonetheless, Orissa had the highest loan default rate of our three states.

The consequence for both Orissa and Tamilnadu was that large, established industries got a disproportionate share of loans and of all other kinds of assistance. Although very few respondents in either of those states got loans at all (4 of 40 in Orissa, 6 of 73 in Tamilnadu), those who did were far more likely to be at the high end of the scale than the low. In contrast, and characteristically, the Punjab government lent all of its money, but only in small quantities. Officially, the maximum allowable loan size there had been set at Rs. 25,000—half the maximum Rs. 50,000 in the other two states. Moreover, almost all of the 22 of 70 respondents in Punjab who took government loans received loans of only Rs. 5,000. Again characteristically, to get a loan, one paid about 6 per cent in *bakhsheesh*.

After a great deal of resistance from the banks, even after nationalization, the central government finally was able to force them to make loans to small industries. In 1971, very few of our respondents had ever taken a bank loan, although many had tried. By 1975, almost all of the larger firms had been able to get some kind of bank assistance, the most common (and least risky for the bank) being bill discounting. Accordingly, their interest in obtaining loans through the Small-Scale Industries Program declined, even though in principle loans from that source were still more attractive than loans from the bank.

Another example of the attempt to rationalize processes is reflected in the creation of two national purchasing and marketing organizations: the State Trading Corporation of India (STC) and the Minerals and Metals Trading Corporation (MMTC) (Gupta, 1971). One rationale for establishing them was to coordinate purchases from abroad and, by processing orders centrally and pooling suppliers, to increase sales of Indian goods abroad. This was particularly desirable, it was argued, for trade with the Eastern bloc countries, where trade was organized government to government, volume was large, and representatives of those countries preferred dealing with other officials to dealing with private entrepreneurs.

From there, it was just a step from coordinating to centralizing purchasing. Why have hundreds of individual manufacturers buy goods or raw materials abroad? Small orders are disadvantaged compared to large ones; bulk purchasing would offer savings. Moreover, the STC and MMTC, by doing most of the international buying and selling, would reduce the amount of illegal manipulation of currencies endemic under the existing individualistic system. From that premise began the program of requiring imported merchandise and materials to be "canalized" through the STC or MMTC respectively, to be purchased domestically from them by individual buyers. A similar process could, it was argued, be instituted for sales.

In principle, this all sounds perfectly reasonable. In practice, the added layer of bureaucracy made buying imported materials harder and more costly than ever before. Some respondents were more than a year behind schedule in receiving their canalized goods. These procedures applied to both large and small industries, although large industries could sometimes avoid them. The STC was never able fully to organize purchases for export in the same way. It got stuck in its own red tape in trying to coordinate thousands of small industries.

The wish to provide whole, totally organized, systems pervaded other programs, even where hostility toward business was not the motive. The government provided booklets describing how to establish new industries by showing in extraordinary detail how to set up a vertically-integrated factory, disregarding the cheaper parts for the finished product readily available in the market. This was particularly disastrous for the new entrepreneur, the person most likely to look at the booklet, both because he might not know which activities were essential and which were not, and because his capital was limited. One informant reported that he had considered buying machinery to make small parts at a cost of Rs. 20,000; he later discovered he could buy the parts as he needed them for Rs. 5 each.

Following the principle of comprehensiveness, the Small Industries Service Institutes tried to offer a little of everything. Management courses, accounting courses, and technical process-related courses abounded. Technical advisers—a kind of industrial extension agent—were assigned to each center as troubleshooters for a wide range of problems. Where there was little demand for services, as in Orissa, the whole establishment languished, taking on the lethargy characteristic of the area. (Small Industries Service Institute officials were central government servants who might have been serving in locations far from their homes. In Orissa, the top official was a Bengali; his assistant was from Uttar Pradesh.) One agent ritualistically printed brochures no-one read and planned classes to which no-one came. Sometimes a young applicant for an Industries Department loan would appear. He thought that if he took the course, he would be showing initiative, and the Director would intervene for him. That did occasionally happen. A pragmatic course of action in this setting—assuming that closing the operation down was not an option—would have been to reduce offerings, concentrating on one or two aspects of the program that might be helpful (although in Orissa it was not easy to tell what those might be).

The Small Industries Service Institutes in Tamilnadu and Punjab suffered from the same overcommitment to comprehensiveness, although the style of each reflected something of the state in which it operated. The building in which the Madras SISI was housed was by far the handsomest and best cared for of the three. Most of its broad corridors and airy classrooms were unused. Reflecting the superior education but limited production skills of the most successful Madrasi small industrialists, it abounded in courses in management. In fact, the Tamilnadu program had more staff specializing in management than any other in India. The Institute offered a series of six-month courses. Respondents who attended them did find them valuable, principally in providing the opportunity to meet other small-scale industrialists, share mutual problems, and make contacts. The courses served as a kind of state supported Rotary Club.

In addition to giving courses, the Madras SISI had a staff of extension agents to help people solve technical problems. According to respondents, all but one of the agents, an expert in electroplating, were inept. Those who sought assistance with any other problem did not receive any. One, in despair, went to the public library, where he found a book that helped him.

In Punjab, both management programs and technical programs limped along with few participants. None of our Punjab respondents ever made use of the SISI for any purpose, believing the management programs were just talk and their own technical skills were superior. One respondent reported he once asked at the SISI if someone could tell him the optimum size of an aperture for a heating fan with a blade of a specified size. No one could. So he experimented by making several apertures of different sizes until he found the one that worked best. One SISI expert on knitted goods was widely respected, although no-one in our sample used his services.

The Punjabi parts manufacturers, aware that their products were not always very precise, pushed for tooling assistance. The Director of the SISI, a South Indian, was trying to raise money for improving the tool shop, whose equipment, in 1975, was outdated. In this, he was working with the state Department of Industries which was, however, engaged in trying to attract large manufacturers to Punjab. To get the Department interested in his problem, he pointed out that the abundance of small-scale machining industries is an attraction to big manufacturers, enabling them to become assemblers by farming out contracts and avoiding investment in costly plants and machinery.

That the program in each area might become more specialized, less comprehensive, and tailored to the particular needs of its constituency was, ironically, seen by officials as a problem. According to the Commissioner for Small-Scale Industries, deviations from equal provision of all program services and facilities were imbalances that had to be rectified. Accidental forces might move the program in one or another direction in various states, but these were temporary deviations; the program, he believed, should be identical in every state.

Programs to encourage small-scale industries have not, then, had much impact on the growth of small industries. The concern with comprehensive organization of systems, coupled with a commitment to equity and a hostility to business as an enterprise, made an excellently conceived program less effective than it otherwise might have been. Even so, small-scale industries in India were growing in number and in the share they provided of total Indian industrial output. Why should that be? Perhaps the most important reason was that the small-scale sector was the freest and most open one in the Indian economy. People could move into small industries both from the larger-scale sectors, which were more regulated and controlled, and from the unindustrialized sector, because access was relatively easy.

In a program designed to offer comprehensive incentives and facilitators to small industry, the best incentive—probably unwittingly—was what omitted: a licensing requirement for small-scale producers. It is difficult to overemphasize the importance of freedom from regulation. Larger-scale enterprises were locked into a system created by rationalistic officials designing a planned economy. To be sure that needed goods were produced, while not wasting scarce resources in the superfluous production of excess quantities, and to insure that raw materials would be available to feed all the machines in which manufacturers had invested, the government established output quotas—maxima, not minima—for virtually every product manufactured in the larger-scale sectors. To assure that output quotas were not exceeded, they further created a system limiting both the maximum capacity of individual plants and the total number of plants permitted to produce a given item. To ensure that manufacturers did not simply decide that because there was a market for a particular product in excess of the government's limitation, they would manufacture more of the product anyway, the government created an elaborate licensing system for manufacturers in the larger-scale sectors. Manufacturers had to apply for permission to produce the desired product, report their capital investment, outline their raw materials resources, and agree to restrict their production to the level they had originally requested the right to produce. An extensive literature documents the problems with this policy (Hazari, 1966 and 1967; Jayaraman, 1971).

Beginning in the early 1970s, the government relaxed some of the most stringent of the licensing procedures. Nonetheless, entry was still restricted to license holders. Any reader of this book can imagine all that went into obtaining a license. Once licensed, one was obliged to restrict output, thereby limiting growth. Once in production, one was required to reapply if one wished to alter modes of production, change product or product mix, or alter raw materials or power requirements. These regulations were a major incentive for a growing small-scale manufacturer to avoid moving out of that sector if at all possible. One respondent whose industry had in fact made the transition from small to medium scale reported he was obliged to keep a full-time representative in New Delhi simply to push paper from office to office. It took him three years to get his medium-scale license.

To maintain the flexibility to change product lines while excluding competitors, many large industrial and commercial groups obtained licenses for goods they had no current intention to produce. Having a license to produce a desired good in a controlled market is like having a license to print money. At a minimum, it guarantees the sale of one's entire output.

No licensing constraints were imposed on the small-scale sector. During the period of raw materials scarcity, many small-scale industrialists did register with the states' industries departments so that they could get materials allocations, and the governments pressed the remainder to register so it could keep track of them. Even this formality, however, was not required.

In other respects, too, small industries were not subject to the same level of control as large industries were. Exemptions from requirements of the Factory Act, as we discussed earlier, and from certain features of the income tax laws, are examples here. We have already seen how large units often set up small subunits precisely to avoid these elements of regulation.

The government may have been willing to relinquish control over small industries simply because there were so many of them that the costs of maintaining close supervision were enormous. In 1972, for example, the Director of Industries in Punjab estimated there were 60,000 small units in his state alone. Nonetheless, at the height of the raw materials shortages in 1971, the Director of Industries in Tamilnadu told us his government was considering a program for licensing new entrants into the metal shaping industries. There were already so many of these very small producers that the problem of supplying them with materials was overwhelming. Moreover, he felt that the market was saturated with their wares. He was probably correct. Whether licensing was the best solution, however, is problematic.

A second factor favoring establishing small industries was a fear that larger-scale enterprises would eventually be nationalized. This was not an irrational fear. Between 1970 and 1975, the Government of India nationalized the Life Insurance Corporation of India, all of the large banks, many of the bus companies, and the Indian Iron and Steel Corporation. Legislation setting ceilings on rural land-holdings was first implemented in the 1950s, but the late 1960s saw both more vigorous enforcement of existing laws and the advent of land ceilings for urban real estate. Rich individuals, concerned to protect their assets, in some cases set up small industries as a shelter for capital. The government's message to industrialists was clear: it watched large industrialists closely but its attitude toward small ones was encouraging. About one-third of the industries in our sample were in fact created by the downward flow of money from upper-income groups seeking less regulation, economic benefit from incentives, and lower visibility.

By 1975, the freedom of small industries to stay completely clear of government intervention was being eroded. Unhappy about the quality of information about the industries that was then available, each state was undertaking business censuses to learn what was happening. As the industries became more numerous and more prosperous, the government was moving in. Regardless of the content of future policy statements enunciating principles for industrial development, the Indian government's disposition toward comprehensive control will not easily be eschewed.

What have small industries achieved with respect to the aspirations the government had for them? Much to the surprise of planners, they are not especially labor intensive. Manufacturers aspired to move from labor to machinery as quickly as possible, because machines are faster, more precise, and less emotional than humans. Even the *gurakhu* manufacturer in our sample was trying to locate a machine to pack the finished product in tins, a job for which he had been using hand labor. It appeared to us the perfect job for low-wage, unskilled labor. Nonetheless, he had expended considerable time and money to find a machine that could pack the thick, viscous stuff. Workers were slower, they required management, and they were less reliable.

Sandesara (1966), using aggregate data, compared labor intensity and productivity between small and large industries within given industrial categories, and concluded:

> The underlying assumption of public policy, in promoting small industrial units in a country like India, seems to be that such units use capital—the scarce resource—sparingly, and labour—the plentiful resource—abundantly in the sense that they

embody a technology which (a) produces more output and leaves more surplus and (b) employs more labour, *each* per unit of capital, as compared to the large-sized units. Actually almost the opposite conclusion appears to be the outcome of our labours. The evidence indicates that in general small units produce less output and leave less surplus, and that very often they also employ fewer persons, *each* per unit of capital than large ones (p. 198, emphasis in original).

Sandesara's findings are not uncontroversial. Census data may underreport the number of workers per unit of capital invested in the small-scale sector, because many of those workers were illegally employed—either because they were too young or because accurately reporting a larger number of workers would bring an enterprise under increased regulation. Nonetheless, Sandesara's point seems correct in general. Certainly, our small-scale industrialists strove always to reduce the amount of labour, relative to capital, that they required.

With respect to the goals of recruiting new entrepreneurial talent and solving directly the rural unemployment problem, small-scale industries are a failure. We have already discussed the unhappy results of efforts to generate rural industry, even in Punjab. However, where agricultural laborers have been willing to migrate, they have found employment opportunity.

Curiously, small industry's positive contributions are not those anticipated by planners, many of whom thought that small industries would be technologically simple, use large quantities of labour, and produce low-quality consumer goods for local consumption. Yet it is clear that most small-scale industries had little interest in producing crude goods for peasants. Indeed, they wanted to be as much like their larger counterparts as possible— only on a smaller scale. The accomplishments of small-scale industries have come as something of a surprise to planners and to some condescending government officials. These accomplishments include high level training in technical skills that upgrades the labor force, a result of reducing costs by hiring young, untrained people and teaching them to operate lathes, grinders, and other factory machinery. In fact, because they do not have jigs and fixtures to assure uniform product quality, workers must become highly skilled to achieve the proper tolerances.

Even excluding those manufacturers whose small firms were a repository for capital from larger enterprises, we find that small-scale industries made a substantial contribution to industrial production. Further, to exclude those individuals may be an excessively stringent requirement in measuring increased output, because using capital to manufacture goods in the small scale may be more productive than other uses of the same capital might be. Omitting them, we find that the remaining 122 firms in our sample reported gross sales of Rs. 31,441,850, almost certainly an understatement; and they provided, for one-sixth of our respondents, the opportunity for dramatic, unambiguous upward mobility.

In 1972, small industries in Punjab alone earned Rs. 300 million in foreign exchange. Small industries were changing the face of India not only in Punjab but in Gujarat and Maharashtra as well. They were making substantial contributions to industrial output in Tamilnadu and West Bengal. There might have been more of them if the government did not try so zealously to help them, because the principal reason many of these small industries were so successful was that the government left them relatively alone.

CHAPTER TWELVE

CONCLUSION

The 192 owners of small-scale industries whom we surveyed in Orissa, Tamilnadu, and Punjab varied widely in their skills, interests, and the types of enterprises they owned. Well-educated sons of wealthy families and uneducated offspring of the poor, producing the most sophisticated goods to the crudest, they varied, too, in their degree of success. At every level of income and education, however, were many who contributed increased production to the Indian economy.

We have shown there is no meaningful way to locate this group at some point along a hypothetical continuum of modernity and tradition, at least as that continuum is commonly thought of. Their lifestyles and attitudes varied as much as their products and their incomes. What they shared was a concern with profit and loss, and the capacity to calculate their interests rationally—a capacity enhanced by the immediacy and clarity of feedback available to them—however they may have behaved outside their business spheres. This hardheaded calculation affected their choices of products to manufacture and product mixes, treatment of labor, approaches to buying raw materials, and marketing strategies.

Although the entrepreneurs differed, they differed in characteristic ways from state to state. Businessmen in Tamilnadu were likely to be well educated and to come from wealthier families than did either Orissans or Punjabis. The Tamilnadu group, on the whole, had fewer technical skills than the Punjabis, and were more averse to taking risks. Orissa businessmen, reflecting their state's lesser industrial development, were more likely to come from commercial families, for whom industry was a sideline, than were those in the other two states. They manufactured low-technology products that appealed to local tastes. About as well educated as the Punjabis, the successful Orissans were more likely to have supportive political ties than were industrialists in either of the other two states. The Tamilnadu and Orissa businessmen were more likely to produce either whole products or fabrications to order than were the Punjabis, who produced highly differentiated goods for a larger, more open market. The Punjabis got the most from both their labor and their machinery, and benefited from a highly specialized division of labor. Conspicuous consumers as compared to the more ascetic groups in Tamilnadu and Orissa, Punjabis were more likely than the others to be upwardly mobile. Orissa was the only one of the three states in which outsiders played a major role in industry. The successful large-scale industries were virtual colonies set down on Orissa soil, in some cases using Orissan raw materials, but staffed and supported from outside the state.

How comparable were these states to others in India? And how comparable were the small industries we studied to others throughout the country? Several hundred thousand small industries were distributed all over India in 1975, concentrated particularly heavily in Punjab, Gujarat, Maharashtra, West Bengal, and Tamilnadu. Of these, Punjab was anomalous because it had industrialized later than the others and had fewer large industries than they. In addition, Partition had deprived it of its major cities. Maharashtra and Gujarat (the two were once combined in a single state) and West Bengal were the first areas in India to develop major industry (Buchanan, 1934). They became important world suppliers respectively of cotton textile and jute products in the late nineteenth century.

Maharashtra and Gujarat resemble Tamilnadu in the pattern of small-scale industry growth. In all three of these states, wealth acquired in other sectors was an important source of investment in small-scale industries, and in all three, some of the newer entrepreneurs had come from the ranks of the educated unemployed. According to Panini, the pattern in the state of Karnataka also resembles the Tamilnadu pattern (personal communication). The shape of small industries in West Bengal, by contrast, most closely resembles that in Punjab. As the Ramgarhias dominated the machining industries in Ludhiana, so the Mahisyas were an almost legendary group of machinists in Howrah, a suburb of Calcutta (Owens, 1970). Unlike Punjab, Tamilnadu, Gujarat, and Maharashtra, West Bengal did not experience explosive growth of small industries in the 1960s and early 1970s. In part, they had begun the 1960s with a more developed small industry base, but in part, chaotic political conditions there undermined production in all the industrial sectors. Finally, the poor industrial performance in Orissa parallels that in other poor Indian states such as Madhya Pradesh.

Indian society and culture are sometimes thought to have placed constraints on industrial growth. Whatever those constraints are supposed to have been, we saw no evidence of them. Entrepreneurial activity was not limited to a few castes or communities. It appeared to be attractive to all who could mobilize the resources. Our data show, not surprisingly, that the lower the entry costs and the fewer the formal rules and regulations, the greater the number of people who started up small industries.

The quantity of entrepreneurship in a society is not fixed. We assume that people are opportunity seekers; accordingly, new information about what is possible, changing systems of constraint, fluctuations in resource availability, and shifts in the psychological climate that generate either optimism or pessimism all influence the expansion or contraction of entrepreneurial activity.

The opportunity structure in India has expanded dramatically since Independence, paralleling the massive development of the economic infrastructure. The Government of India has invested vast resources in altering the landscape and, consequently, in altering economic possibilities. Paved roads outside of cities doubled, from 98,000 miles to 192,000, between 1951 and 1971. Electricity production in the same period rose tenfold, from 5,858 million to 55,828 million kilowatt hours. Raw material production also increased dramatically: pig iron production, for example, increased from 1,735,000 to 6,740,000 tons. We need not elaborate on how such growth alters the structure of possibilities for those who want to make money.

At the same time, the population has become much more educated. The proportion of literate people almost doubled, and the number of schools and colleges almost tripled. For the educated, government employment was, in the immediate post-Independence period, the occupation of choice. Government employment became less attractive, however, as salaries in other sectors began to catch up, and as the electorate, through its political representatives, narrowed the latitude previously given to members of the administrative civil service (Taub, 1969). In our 1963 research, we found that most officials did not aspire to government service for their children, but were training them to be engineers. So, as it turned out, was everyone else. By 1968, the country was glutted with engineers. For most, government employment was virtually the only employment available. In this period, unemployment among the educated more generally became a critical problem. Not only could arts graduates not find jobs, a common pattern throughout much of the Third World, but neither could engineers or even doctors.

Tamilnadu was particularly hard hit by these developments, for two reasons. First, Tamilians have historically been massively over-represented in the all-India government services. Tamilnadu had an unusually good, English-style educational system and maintained the use of English (in part to fight the acceptance of Hindi as the national language). Consequently, Tamilians, more than others, had been successful in the examinations required for most government posts. With growing anti-Brahmin sentiment in South India backed by increasing political muscle, Brahmins found it harder to get either seats in professional schools or government jobs. With one avenue of opportunity closed, they began to look for others. In the South, for Brahmin and non-Brahmin alike, small industry became an increasingly attractive option. Nonetheless, people in Tamilnadu are less adventurous and risk-taking than Punjabis. Their preference for guaranteed profit may in some measure be product of the orientation that found government jobs so desirable.

Government activities, then, have altered the Indian opportunity structure, while social factors in Tamilnadu have affected individual responses to that changing structure. The government has improved the infrastructure, increasing opportunities for all kinds of industry, large or small. Its system of controls on the larger-scale industrial sectors has driven some investors to the small. It created educational opportunities that rapidly outran opportunities for state employment. To the extent that small industry success was increasingly visible in Tamilnadu, more people considered it an option. Gossip and shared information about successful small industries and industrialists circulated among the middle class in Madras during our stay, increasing the visibility of small industries and fueling the growth in their attractiveness. Everyone had a relative who was trying small industry.

In Orissa, the dynamic was the same for some. Holders of commercial wealth gave industry a tentative try to see if it would be a new source of prosperity. Poverty was so widespread, however, that local markets were not yet large enough to sustain substantial industrial growth. For the educated in Orissa, government and university employment was not quite the closed door that it was in Tamilnadu or Punjab. Education lagged behind that available elsewhere in India for so long that higher-ranking government posts, available engineering positions, and chairs in colleges and universities historically had gone to outsiders. By 1975, outsiders were yielding to the local people under increased pressure, endemic to India, for "sons of the soil" to hold local posts, and there was more room in Orissa than elsewhere to employ the educated. Still, people from Orissa did not yet know how to be industrialists—or any other kind of businessmen, for that matter. If growing up in a business environment makes it easier to learn how to do business, growing up where there is virtually none makes learning how very difficult. Oriyas tried to establish industries. Unlike the Bengalis, Marwaris, Gujaratis and Punjabis in Orissa, they often failed. Industrialists relied on political sponsorship to succeed, because they had not developed the skills to maintain an ongoing enterprise. They had neither the advantages of education that characterized many in Tamilnadu, the experience of dealing with finance that characterized some of the commerical families, nor the advantages of previous industrial experience characteristic of the Punjabis. Our Orissa sample included only one indigenous Oriya machinist. He went to Calcutta, where he learned to operate lathes, grinders, and drill presses. He returned to Orissa with some worn, second-hand Bengali machines and, with almost no capital, set up an industry repairing metal objects. He earned a living, but nothing in his environment encouraged him. His family were all agriculturalists, owning an acre here or a half acre there. No other member of his family had ever left the farm. His caste had not entered industry at all. The Punjabi machinists in Orissa did better, partly because they had previous industrial experience, partly because most of their friends and relatives had, too. They traveled between Punjab and Orissa for weddings and holidays, and they brought back relatives to work with them. For some purposes, education and experience may be almost interchangeable; but without either, opportunities for success are severely limited.

Significantly, the two successful Orissans in our sample who had neither political support nor family wealth were carrying on family traditions. The biscuit maker's family had a small candy factory and shop. He then worked as a wholesale grocer, and learned something about the structure of an ongoing business. Like the Punjabis, he too reported that his product wasn't good, but it was getting better all the time; like them, too, he devoted a good deal of energy to learning what he needed to know to make it better. The second was the owner of the *chitralaya*, hardly an industry at all, who was inventing new products and developing procedures for reducing the time that his stocks were idle.

Turning to Punjab, we have seen how the structure of both industry and environment there facilitated entry at all levels, making industry an option for a wide range of people, even those of limited means. We have also seen how, once such a process is set in motion, an atmosphere is created that feeds on itself, encouraging new people to try. The elaborated division of labor, the availability of markets, the atmosphere of success, and the affluence that creates new markets all contributed to an ongoing system that facilitated industrial activity.

To say all this, however, is to beg the prior question of how such systems—indeed, how any systems—are set in motion. The question of origins is very different from that of maintenance of structures and systems once they have become established, a question that has vexed sociologists and to which few satisfactory answers have yet been provided. Perhaps this is because origins are always, at bottom, idiosyncratic; chance combinations of elements build on each other to form things that, over time, take on system characteristics that then tend to maintain themselves as systems. This may be why it is so difficult, in some instances, to create structures and systems whole, on the basis of existing models. If all of Orissa could be transplanted to Punjab, would Orissans become successful industrialists? We don't know. We can, however, look toward the system of constraints introduced into the environment by government activity toward industry. If one is interested in the introduction of values into the industrialization process, this is an important place to begin. A high level of control, especially in the service of conflicting values and goals, some of them inimical to the success of industry, will discourage many; only those with resources and determination will be able to succeed, and then probably through particularistic networks and an ability to play the system off against itself.

Of the three state governments, the Punjab government is the one most willing to look the other way. This makes it possible for all enterprisers to devote full time to making and selling their product, a facility that is particularly crucial to the small industrialist, who cannot afford the personnel to manage the bookkeeping and form-filling that compliance with copious rules requires. If the government of India can resist the impulse either to help or hinder by intervention; and can continue to provide industrial peace and improve the infrastructure, particularly in those areas where growth is taking place; and if agricultural production can be sustained, providing a reasonable level of purchasing power for much of the population; the process of growth in the small-scale industrial sector will continue. It will not matter whether the new entrepreneurs are modern or traditional men; rather, much will depend on whether they have a chance to try without undue artificial constraint.

APPENDIX

SMALL INDUSTRIES QUESTIONNAIRE

First, I would like to ask you some questions about yourself and your background.

1 What is your age?
2 To which community do you belong? (Include location, caste, subcaste).
3 Does your family have a place which they consider to be the native place or ancestral home? (If no, skip to question 7).
4 Where is it? (Give state, village name, near what city?).
5 Did you live there while you were growing up? (If no): Where did you live?
6 Do your parents, brothers, or other relations live there now? (If "other relations," specify).
7 How much education have you had? (Up to what standard?) (If not beyond matric, skip to question 10).
8 At what college or university did you read?
9 What subject(s)?
10 Are you married? (If no, skip to question 17).
11 What is your wife's age?
12 For how many years have you been married?
13 Do you have any children? (If no, skip to question 17.)
14 Can you tell me the sex and age of each?
15 (For grown children): Can you tell me how much education each one has had? AND/OR (For young children): Can you tell me how much education each one will have?
16 (a) (For grown children): What occupation does each one have? AND/OR (For young children): What occupation are you planning for each one?
   (b) (If daughters are there): Can you tell me the occupations of your sons-in-law? AND/OR what occupations would you choose for prospective sons-in-law?
17 Besides yourself, who else lives in your house most of the year? (Include nonrelatives, such as friend, paying guest, servant, etc.) (For relatives, state precise relationship.)
18 What was your father's occupation or occupations while you were growing up?
19 Did he ever have more than one occupation at the same time? (If yes, specify.)
20 Did you have any other occupation before you got into this particular industry?
21 (If yes to 20): What was your occupation before you got into industry?
22 How did you first decide to get into industry?
23 When did you first decide to get into industry?

24 (If respondent is founder): How did you decide to set up this particular industry?

25 When did you decide to set up this particular industry?

26 Did anyone give you advice?

27 Are any members of your immediate family (father, brothers, etc.) in business with you? (Specify number and relationship.)

28 Do you have any (other) relatives in commerce or industry? (Specify.) (If no, skip to question 30).

29 What do they do?

30 Do you have any (other) partners in your business? (Speficy number and relationship to respondent if any).

31 Do you own any industries other than this one? (If no, skip to question 34).

32 Can you tell me what each one is, where it is located, and whether or not it is also a small-scale industry?

33 (If yes to 32): Why do you prefer having several small-scale industries to having a single larger-scale industry?

34 Approximately how much capital did you need to start your industry for:
Land _____ Buildings _____ Machinery _____
Raw materials _____ Other (specify) _____

35 Approximately what is your capital investment now?

36 Where did you get your capital?
Bank _____ Own savings _____
Cooperative society _____ Private loans (family, friends) _____
Family gift _____ State Financial Corporation _____
Life Insurance Corp. _____ Other (specify) _____
Moneylender _____

37 How many employees do you have?

38 How many of them are supervisors?

39 How many (or, what proportion) of them are skilled workers?

40 How many (or, what proportion) of them are unskilled workers?

41 If you require workers, how do you go about obtaining them?

42 Have you ever obtained workers from (if not mentioned in 41):
Employment exchange _____
Jobbers _____
Other workers _____
State Industrial Training Institute _____

43 Is your industry an ancillary industry? (If no, skip to question 47).

44 To which major industry are you attached?

45 What proportion of your output goes to your major industry?

46 (If 45 is less than 100%): Does the rest of your output go to the market? (If industry is ancillary—yes to question 43—skip to question 50).

47 Do you produce mainly on contract, or mainly for the market?

48 Do you have any principal purchasers of your product? (If yes, specify).

49 (If yes): Do they usually pay their bills promptly?

50 What was your company's turnover [gross revenue] last year?

51 Did your business show a profit last year? (If no, skip to question 53)

52 How much, as reported on your income tax?

53 Do you have income from other sources than your business? (If yes, specify, e.g., family lands, real estate, etc.)

54 Do you require any licenses or essentiality certificates for your business? (If yes, specify.) (If no, skip to question 56).

55 How much time did it take between making application for your licence(s) and receiving it (them)?

56 Do you export your product?

57 Do you use any materials which are under government control? (If no, skip to question 60).

58 Which one(s)?

59 How much time does it usually take between applying for your allocation(s) and receiving it (them)?

60 Do you purchase on the black market?

61 Have you experienced any particular difficulties in running your business to your satisfaction? (If yes, specify).

62 Would you say that your business has been expanding, remaining about the same, or becoming less?

63 What are your business plans for the future? (E.g., expansion of plant, change of product line, setting up new small-scale industry, etc.)

64 Is your industry registered as a small-scale industry? (If no): Is there some reason why you have not registered? (If yes): Why did you register?

65 If you became very prosperous, what would you do with your money?

66 Suppose a young man of your caste with money to invest came to you for advice on starting a small industry. (a) What would you tell him to look for? (b) What would you tell him to avoid?

67 Suppose you were manufacturing a product and you had no marketing arrangements for it. Suppose you could do one of two things, either (a) obtain a contract for the sale of your total output, at a very low rate of profit per unit, or (b) Compete in the open market, with the possibility of making a much higher profit per unit but with no guarantee about the volume of your sales. Which of these alternatives would you choose?

Now I want to ask you a few questions about your contacts with govenment.

68 Have you utilized any government assistance or services in the operation of your industry? (If no, skip to question 76).

69 Which ones?

70 What steps did you have to go through to get assistance from government?

71 Did government require you to do anything (e.g., put up capital, take training courses, etc.) before providing the assistance you required? (If yes, specify).

72 How much time did it take for you to get the assistance you requested?

73 Approximately how many government officers have you had to deal with in utilizing government services?

74 Can you remember what their positions were?

75 Which government departments, corporations, and/or institutes have you had dealings with?

76 What (other) government assistance and information programs for small-scale industries are available that you know about, even if you haven't used them personally?

77 Have you ever applied to government for assistance and been turned down? (If no, skip to question 79).

78 Can you give me details of what happened? (Type of assistance applied for, amount of loan if any, number of officers seen, reasons given for rejection, amount of time between application and rejection, etc.).

79 Have you ever applied to government for a license and been turned down? (If no, skip to question 81).

80 Can you give me the details of what happened?

81 Have you ever applied to government for allocation of controlled materials and been turned down? (If no, skip to question 83).

82 Can you give me the details of what happened?

83 How did you first learn that government had programs to assist small-scale industrialists?

84 How did you first come into contact with a government official in regard to your business?

85 What additional services for helping small industrialists would you like to see government provide?

86 Do any programs or requirements of government hinder the efficient conduct of your business? (If no, skip to question 89.)

87 Which one(s)?

88 How does it (do they) interfere?

89 Government officials in Industries Departments and Small-Scale Industries Services Institutes often say that their major responsibility is to help small industries succeed. Do you feel that this is their attitude? (If yes, skip to question 91.)

90 What do you find their attitude to be? (What do you think they are doing?)

Finally, I would like to shift from questions about your contacts with government, and ask your opinions on some general questions.

91 How would you rank the following occupations in terms of the respect you give them?

Agriculturist _____	Doctor _____
Lawyer _____	IAS Officer _____
Moneylender _____	Manufacturer _____
Trader _____	School teacher _____
Priest _____	

92 Would you say that you are more religious or less religious than most of your friends?

93 (a) Some people say that astrology is a science much like any other. Many people may practice it who have not mastered its principles, and thus many errors may come in. But if we really understood the principles rightly, then predictions based on astrology would be correct 100% of the time.

(b) Some people say, we may not know if astrology is scientific or not, but when practiced by a really good astrologer, it is striking how often his predictions come true.

(c) Some people say that astrology has no scientific basis. If we look at predictions based on astrology carefully, we find they are wrong at least as often as they are right.

Which of these three views most closely represents your own?

94 (For Hindus only):

(a) Some people say that airplanes, tanks, and radios are modern inventions.
(b) Others say that they are actually quite ancient; evidence for their existence many centuries back can be found in Ramayana and Mahabharata.

Which view do you think is correct?

95 (a) Some people say that all events and experiences we have in the world have a rational explanation, even though science may not yet be advanced enough to provide that explanation.
(b) Other people say that science may be there, but ghosts, spirits, and other supernatural agencies are still very much with us, and it is only through recognizing their action that we will ever be able to understand certain seemingly unexplainable events.

Which view do you think is correct?

96 (a) Some people say that educating one's daughter beyond reading, writing, and arithmetic is a waste of money.
(b) Some people say that nowadays girls must have more education than formerly, but sons must still be given the most because they must make their way in the world.
(c) Some people say that nowadays it is just as necessary for a daughter to have education as it is for a son.

Which of these views do you think is correct?

97 (For respondents with children only.) (a) One father says, "When my son grows up, I expect that he will live more comfortably than his mother and I are living today."
(b) One father says, "When my son grows up, he will probably live about as comfortably as his mother and I are living today."
(c) One father says, "When my son grows up, he will be lucky if he lives even as comfortably as his mother and I are living today."

Which of these fathers is most like you?

98 (a) One man says, "The most important thing a twelve-year-old boy should learn to do is always obey the wishes of his elders."
(b) Another man says, "The most important thing a boy should learn is to think for himself."

Which man do you think is correct?

99 A boy had to leave school once for lack of money. The only job he could find was of a bearer in a hotel.
(a) One uncle told him, "Work as a bearer and save your money. Then you will be able to go back to school."
(b) The other uncle told him, "It is beneath your position to be a bearer. It is better for you to give up your ideas of study rather than to be a bearer."

Which uncle do you think was correct?

100 (a) One man says, "One must work hard in order to have better results."
(b) A second man says, "One must work hard, but the results are in God's hands."
(c) A third man says, "One need not work hard, because the results are in God's hands."

Which of these men do you think is correct?

101 (a) One learned man says, "When people compete with each other, they work

harder and do their best, and there is progress."

(b) Another learned man says, "When people compete with each other, they become enemies, and progress is impossible."

Which of these two learned men do you think is correct?

Thank you very much.

REFERENCES

Adorno, Theodor W., *et al.*
   1950   *The Authoritarian Personality.* New York: Harper.
Ahmed, Fakhruddin Ali
   n.d. (ca. 1968) "Growth of Small-Scale Industry in India" in
           Government of India, Development Commissioner,
           Small-Scale Industries, *Small-Scale Industries in India.*
           New Delhi.
Alexander, P.C.
   n.d. (ca. 1968) "The Indian Programme for Development of
           Small-Scale Industries—Some Strong Points" in Govern-
           ment of India, Development Commissioner, Small-Scale
           Industries, *Small-Scale Industries in India.* New Delhi.
Andreski, Stanislav
   1968   "Method and Substantive Theory in Max Weber" in S.N.
           Eisenstadt, ed., *The Protestant Ethic and Modernization.*
           New York: Basic Books.
Bell, Daniel
   1960   *The End of Ideology.* Glencoe: The Free Press.
Bendix, Reinhard
   1964   *Nation Building and Citizenship.* New York: Wiley.
Berna, J.J.
   1960   *Industrial Entrepreneurship in Madras State.* Bombay:
           Asia Publishing House.
Broehl, Wayne G., Jr.
   1978   *The Village Entrepreneur: Change Agents in India's Rural
           Development.* Cambridge: Harvard University Press.
Buchanan, Daniel H.
   1934   *The Development of Capitalistic Enterprise in India.* New
           York: Macmillan.

Cantril, Hadley
  1965 *Patterns of Human Concern.* Rutgers: Rutgers University Press.

Cole, Arthur H.
  1959 *Business Enterprise in its Social Setting.* Cambridge: Harvard University Press.
  1965 "An Approach to the Study of Entrepreneurship" in Hugh G. J. Aitken, ed., *Explorations in Enterprise.* Cambridge: Harvard University Press.

Deshpande, Manohar U.
  1982 *Entrepreneurship of Small-Scale Industries.* New Delhi: Deep and Deep Publications.

Deshpande, Sudha and Deshpande, L. K.
  1985 "Census of 1981 and the Structure of Employment" in *Economic and Political Weekly,* Bombay, Vol. XX, No. 22 (June 1), 969–73.

Eldersveld, Samuel J., V. Jagannadham, and A.P. Barnabas
  1968 *The Citizen and the Administrator in a Developing Democracy.* Glenview: Scott, Foresman.

Feuer, Lewis Samuel
  1969 *Conflict of Generations: The Character and Significance of Student Movements.* New York: Basic Books.

Ford Foundation
  1955 *International Planning Team Report on Small Industries in India.* New Delhi: Government of India, Ministry of Commerce and Industry.
  1963 *Development of Small-Scale Industries in India: Prospects, Problems, and Politics—Report of the International Perspective Planning Team.* New Delhi: Government of India, Ministry of Industry.

Ford Foundation, Calcutta Metropolitan Planning Organization
  1969 *Basic Development Plan for the Calcutta Metropolitan District, 1966-1986.* Calcutta: Government of West Bengal.
  1973 Personal communication.

Germani, Gino
  1969 "Secularization, Modernization, and Economic Development" in S.N. Eisenstadt, ed., *The Protestant Ethic and Modernization.* New York: Basic Books.

Gerschenkrohn, Alexander
  1962 *Economic Backwardness in Historical Perspective.* Cambridge: Belknap Press of Harvard University.

1968   *Continuity in History and other Essays.* Cambridge: Belknap Press of Harvard University

Gilbert, Doris C., and D.J. Levinson
1956   "Ideology, Personality, and Institutional Policy in the Mental Hospital" in *Journal of Abnormal and Social Psychology,* Vol. 53, 263–71.

Glazer, Nathan, and Daniel Patrick Moynihan
1963   *Beyond the Melting Pot.* Cambridge: M.I.T. Press.

Goode, William
1963   *World Revolution and Family Patterns.* New York: The Free Press.

Government of India
1948   *Constituent Assembly of India (Legislative) Debates* V (6th–10th April 1948). New Delhi. |
1970   *India Pocket Book of Economic Information.* New Delhi: Ministry of Finance.
1971a   *Census of India.* New Delhi.
1971b   *Preliminary Census Reports.* New Delhi.
1972   *Report of the Banking Commission.* New Delhi.

Government of India,| Development Commissioner Small-Scale Industries
n.d.a (ca. 1968)   *Small-Scale Industries in India.* New Delhi.
n.d.b (ca. 1971)   *Small-Scale Industries.* New Delhi.

Government of India, Planning Commission
1956   *Programmes of Industrial Development|1956–61.* Delhi Government of India Press.
1971   *Annual Plan:|1970–71.* New Delhi.

Government of Madras
1965   *Directory of Small-Scale Industrial Units in Madras State.* 2nd ed. Madras. Director of Industries and Commerce.

Government of Orissa
1967   *Directory of Industries.* Cuttack.
n.d. (ca. 1981)   *Economic Survey of Orissa1980–1981.* Cuttack: Bureau of Statistics and Economics.

Government of Punjab
1965   *Directory of Small-Scale Industrial Units Registered with Directorate of Industries, Punjab.* Chandigarh: Directorate of Industries, Punjab.

Government of Tamilnadu
1965   *See* Government of Madras.
1969   *Directory of Small-Scale Industrial Units in Tamilnadu: Suppliment to the Second Edition.* Madras: Director of

Industries and Commerce.

1982 *Industrial Policy and Programs (Rural and Small Industries), 1982-83.* Madras Industries Department.

Gupta, K.R.

1970 *Working of State Trading in India.* New Delhi: S. Chand.

Hagan, Everett E.

1971 "How Economic Growth Begins" in Peter Kilby, ed., *Entrepreneurship and Economic Development.* New York: The Free Press.

Hazari, R.K.

1966 *Industrial Planning and Licensing Policy: Interim Report to the Planning Commission.* Delhi: Manager of Publications.

1967 *Industrial Planning and Licensing Policy: Final Report.* Delhi: Government of India, Planning Commission.

Hazlehurst, Leighton W.

1968 "Caste and Merchant Communities" in Milton Singer and Bernard S. Cohn, eds., *Structure and Change in Indian Society.* Chicago: Aldine.

Heckscher, Eli

1935 *Mercantilism.* London: Allen and Unwin.

Hoselitz, Bert F.

1968 Preface to Bert F. Hoselitz, ed., *The Role of Small Industry in the Process of Economic Growth.* The Hague: Mouton.

Inkeles, Alex, and David H. Smith

1974 *Becoming Modern,* Cambridge: Harvard University Press.

Jayaraman, T.V.

1971 *Industrial Licensing Policy.* Bombay: Economic Research and Training Foundation.

Kapp, K. William

1963 *Hindu Culture, Economic Development, and Economic Planning in India.* New York: Asia Publishing House.

Lambert, Richard D.

1963 *Workers, Factories, and Social Change in India.* Princeton: Princeton University Press.

Lerner, Daniel

1964 *The Passing of Traditional Society.* Glencoe: The Free Press.

Levy, Marion J., Jr.

1966 *Modernization and the Structure of Society.* Princeton: Princeton University Press.

Lieberson, Stanley
    1963   *Ethnic Patterns in American Cities.* New York: Free Press
            of Glencoe.
Malamud, Bernard
    1957   *The Assistant.* New York: Farrar, Straus, and Cudahy.
Malinowski, Bronislaw
    1954 | *Magic, Science, and Religion and Other Essays.* New York:
            Doubleday.
Marsh, Robert Mortimer
    1967   *Comparative Sociology: A Codification of Cross-Societal
            Analysis.* New York: Harcourt, Brace, and World.
Mayer, Kurt B., and Sidney Goldstein
    1961   *The First Two Years: Problems of Small Firm Growth and
            Survival.* Washington: Small Business Administration.
McClelland, David C.
    1968   "The Impulse to Modernization" in Myron Weiner, ed.,
            Modernization. New York: Basic Books.
McClelland, David C., and David G. Winter
    1968   *Motivating Personal Achievement.* New York: The Free
            Press.
McCrory, James T.
    1956   *Small Industry in a North Indian Town.* Delhi: Ministry of
            Commerce and Industry, Government of India.
Moore, Barrington, Jr.
    1966   *The Social Origins of Dictatorship and Democracy.* Bos-
            ton: Beacon Press.
Morris, Morris David
    1965   *The Emergence of an Industrial Labor Force in India.*
            Berkeley: University of California Press.
Myers, Charles A.
    1958   *Labor Problems in the Industrialization of India.* Cam-
            bridge: Harvard University Press.
Nafziger, E. Wayne
    1973   *Class, Caste and Entrepreneurship: A Study of Indian
            Industrialists.* Honolulu: The University Press of Hawaii.
Nagaraj, R.
    1984   "Subcontracting in Indian Manufacturing Industries:
            Analysis, Evidence and Issues." *Economic and Political
            Weekly,* Vol. XIX, Nos. 31, 32, 33 (August), pp. 1441–43.
Nanjappa, K.L.
    n.d. (ca. 1968)   Introduction to *Small-Scale Industries in India.*
            New Delhi: Government of India, Development Commis-

sioner, Small-Scale Industries.

Okkawa, Kazushi, and Henry Rosovsky
1973 *Japanese Economic Growth.* Stanford: Stanford University Press.

Owens, Raymond Lee
1970 *Peasant Entrepreneurs in a North Indian Industrial City.* Unpublished Ph.D. dissertation, University of Chicago.

Parsons, Talcott
1961 "Differentiation and Variation in Social Structures" in Talcott Parsons, Edward Shils, Kaspar Naegele, and Jesse Pitts, eds., *Theories of Society.* New York: The Free Press.

Portes, Alejandro
1973 "The Factorial Structure of Modernity: Empirical Replications and a Critique" in *American Journal of Sociology,* Vol. 69, No. 1.

Rice, A.K.
1958 *Productivity and Social Organization.* London: Tavistock.

Rose, Arnold
1970 "Sociological Factors Influencing Economic Development in India" in Monte Palmer, ed., *The Human Factor in Economic Development.* Waltham: Ginn.

Ross, Martin
1972 "Family Organization and the Development of Agrarian Capitalism in a North Indian Village." Unpublished manuscript.

Roy, A.K.
n.d. (ca. 1968) "Small Industries Assistance Programme in India" in *Small-Scale Industries in India.* New Delhi: Government of India, Development Commissioner, Small-Scale Industries.

Sandesara, J.C.
1966 "Scale and Technology in Indian Industry" in *Oxford University Institute of Economics and Statistics Bulletin,* Vol. 28, No. 1, 181–98.

Schumpeter, Joseph A.
1942 *Capitalism, Socialism, and Democracy.* New York: Harper.

Shinohara, Miyohei
1968 "Japan" in Bert F. Hoselitz, ed., *The Role of Small Industry in the Process of Economic Growth.* The Hague: Mouton.

Shupe, Anson D., and Lawrence E. Hazelrigg
   1976   "Estimates of Father-to-Son Occupational Mobility in India, Circa 1962." Unpublished manuscript.
Singer, Milton
   1973   *When a Great Tradition Modernizes.* New York: Praeger.
Singer, Milton, and Bernard S. Cohn, eds.
   1968   *Structure and Change in Indian Society.* Chicago: Aldine.
Stern, G.G., M.I. Stein, and B.S. Bloom
   1956   *Methods in Personality Assessment.* Glencoe: The Free Press.
Srinivasan, S.
   1970   *Industrial Estates in India.* Bombay: Vora.
Sundaram, C.R.
   n.d. (ca. 1968)   "The NSIC: Its Programme & Assistance" in *Small-Scale Industries in India.* New Delhi: Government of India, Development Commissioner, Small-Scale Industries.
Taub, Richard P.
   1969   *Bureaucrats Under Stress.* Berkeley: University of California Press.
Taub, Richard P., and Doris L. Taub
   1974   "Small-Scale Industries in Three Indian States: A Report on Work in Progress" in *Fulbright Newsletter,* Summer.
Tyabji, Nasir
   1984   "Nature of Small Enterprise Development: Political Aims and Socio-Economic Reality." *Economic and Political Weekly,* Vol. XIX, Nos. 31, 32, 33 (August), 1425–33.
Venkataraman, R.
   n.d. (ca. 1968) "Role of Planning in Development of Small Industries in India" in *Small-Scale Industries in India,* New Delhi: Government of India, Development Commissioner, Small-Scale Industries.
Vepa, Ram K.
   1971   *Small Industry in the Seventies.* New Delhi: Vikas.
   1983   *Small Industry Development Program.* New Delhi: Indian Institute of Public Administration.
Verba, Sidney, Bashiruddin Ahmed, and Anil Bhatt
   1971   *Caste, Race, and Politics: A Comparative Study of India and the United States.* Beverly Hills: Sage.
Vidich, Arthur J., and Joseph Bensman
   1960   *Small Town in Mass Society.* Garden City: Doubleday Anchor Books.

Wax, Rosalie.
    1973   *Doing Field Work*. Chicago: University of Chicago Press.
Weber, Max
    1958a *The Protestant Ethic and the Spirit of Capitalism*. New York: Scribner.
    1958b *The Religion of India*. Glencoe: The Free Press.
White, Winston
    1961   *Beyond Conformity*. New York: Free Press of Glencoe.

Index